The Best Men's
Stage Monologues 2018

D0556718

Edited and with a Foreword
by Lawrence Harbison

Smith and Kraus Publishers

A Smith and Kraus Book
177 Lyme Road, Hanover, NH 03755
editorial 603.643.6431 To Order 1.877.668.8680
www.smithandkraus.com

The Best Men's Stage Monologues 2018

Manufactured in the United States of America

ISBN: 9781575259260

Library of Congress Control Number: 2329-2709

Typesetting and layout by Elizabeth E. Monteleone

Cover by Olivia Monteleone

For information about custom editions, special sales,
education and corporate purchases,
please contact Smith and Kraus at editor@smithandkraus.com or
603.643.6431.

THE BEST MEN'S
STAGE MONOLOGUES 2018

ACKNOWLEDGEMENTS

Thanks to the following press agents for allowing me to see productions they represented during the 2017-2018 theatre season: Molly Barnett, Mike Borkowski, Scott Braun, Shane Brown, Philip Carruba, Melissa Cohen, Alexandra Cutler, Tom D'Ambrosio, Daniel Demello, Michelle Farabaugh, Glenna Freedman, David Gersten, David Gibbs, Whitney Gore, Karen Greco, Jackie Green, Kelly Guiod, Dale Heller, Richard Hillman, Ailsa Hoke, Judy Jacksina, Jessica Johnson, Michael Jorgenson, Alana Karpoff, Amy Kass, Amanda Kaus, Bridget Klapinski, Scott Klein, Richard Kornberg, Ron Lasko, Kevin McAnarney, Aaron Meier, Miguel Mendiola, Logan Metzler, Shayne Miller, Chelsea Nachman, Brett Charles, Emily Owens, Leslie Papa, Joe Perrotta, Matt Polk, Imani Punch, Jim Randolph, Philip Rinaldi, Lily Robinson, Katie Rosin, Matt Ross, Sam Rudy, Susan Schulman, Sarah Sgro, Paul Siebold, Rachael Singer, Jonathan Slaff, Don Summa, Don Summa, Joe Trentacosta, Wayne Wolfe, Samantha Wolfin, Molly Wyatt, John Wyczniewski, Billy Zavelson and Blake Zidell; and to the following literary agents who granted me rights to include their clients' work in this anthology: Beth Blickers, Jonathan Mills, Amy Wagner, Rachel Viola, Mark Orsini, Alexis Williams, Mary Harden, Charles Koppelman, Amy Mellman, Di Glazer, Olivier Sultan, Mark Subias, Antje Oegel, Susan Gurman, Leah Hamos and Ally Shuster.

Thanks, too, to Amy Marsh of Samuel French, Inc., Peter Hagan of Dramatists Play Service and Christopher Gould of Broadway Play Publishing for sending me plays to read.

And, thanks most of all to the playwrights who sent me their plays.

TABLE OF CONTENTS

FOREWORD

Here you will find a rich and varied selection of monologues for men, most of which are from plays which were produced and/or published in the 2017-2018 theatrical season. Many are for younger performers (teens through 30s) but there are also some excellent pieces for older men as well. The age of the character is indicated in each monologue, but you will find that many may be done by actors of different ages. Some are comic (laughs), some are dramatic (generally, no laughs). Some are rather short, some are rather long. All represent the best in contemporary playwriting.

Several of the monologues are by playwrights whose work may be familiar to you, such as Don Nigro, Aaron Posner, Dominique Morisseau, Richard Nelson, C.S. Hanson, Leslye Headland and Richard Dresser; others are by exciting up-and-comers such as Paola Lázaro, Tanya Saracho, Chelsea Marcentel, Sandra A. Daley-Sharif, Susan Eve Haar, Barret O'Brien and David MacGregor. Many of the plays from which these monologues have been culled have been published and, hence, are readily available either from the publisher/licensor or from a theatrical book store such as the Drama Book Shop in New York. Some may not be published for a while, in which case contact the author or his agent to request a copy of the entire text of the play which contains the monologue which suits your fancy. Information on publishers/rights holders may be found in the Rights & Permissions section in the back of this anthology.

Break a leg in that audition! Knock 'em dead in class!

Lawrence Harbison

MONOLOGUES

AIRNESS
Chelsea Marcantel

Dramatic
Facebender, 30s-40s

*After Nina, a newcomer to competitive air guitar,
trashes the sport and its competitors, she tries to
apologize. Facebender, a veteran of the circuit,
attempts to make her understand what air guitar
means to him and to his friends by telling her about
his job.*

FACEBENDER

Well, it was a match made in heaven. Nobody wants that job,
and at the time, nobody wanted me. I was bumming around,
couldn't find anything steady. Had run up some sizeable
debts. I heard about this job from a buddy, and it sounded
easy enough, so I applied. And I got it. You basically just
have to be willing to walk into disgusting apartments. Sometimes we have to wear hazmat suits and bootees. These people
can be dead for weeks, or months, before anyone finds them.
Before anyone cares. Sometimes there are flies, or roaches,
or mice. Lots of times, people's apartments are just full of
wall-to-wall junk. This one lady last year, died standing up
and stayed that way. There wasn't room in her place to fall
over. We work in pairs, to keep us from stealing. It's weird,
seeing what strangers kept in their closets, what they ate, what
movies they watched, what kind of toilet paper they used. We
go through everything, looking for signs of relationships. Is
there an address book? A business card? A computer? Who
are the people in these photographs? Are they still alive, would
they care that this person is dead? It's the most depressing kind
of archeology, but somebody has to do it. And that somebody
in San Diego County has been me, for the last few years. I've

been through a lot of partners. But I'll tell you one thing. When I die, somebody is gonna know. Right away. Lots of people. I used to go through my life like I was gonna live forever, but now I know. It could be any day. But I won't go out anonymous. No stranger is going to have to pick through my stuff, wondering if there's anybody out in the world who'd care to inherit the $300 in my bank account. Before I started playing air guitar, I hadn't seen my daughter, or her mother, in like six years. I felt like too much time had passed, and I was embarrassed to reach out to them. Now, we hang out at least once a month. It's awkward as fuck, but it's happening. It's getting there. My list of friends gets longer and longer. I text them every day. I hug them every time I see them. When I die, there are gonna be so many broken-hearted motherfuckers, playing sad, sad air guitar solos at my funeral. I put it in my will. I look death in its nasty face every day. And then at night, I come here, and I get up onstage and *live* like there's no tomorrow. Because there isn't. There really isn't. It's silly and it's fun and it's absurd, but life is a slow march off a cliff into nothingness, so why not be as silly as you want?

For information on this author,
click on the WRITERS tab at www.smithandkraus.com

AIRNESS
Chelsea Marcantel

Dramatic
Shreddy Eddie, 20-30s

Shreddy Eddy, a seasoned air guitar competitor, takes offense when newcomer Nina questions his song choice. Shreddy explains to Nina the amount of blood, sweat, and heart it takes to pick the perfect performance song, and become an air guitar champion.

SHREDDY

Grraaah! Have you learned nothing? Am I, Shreddy Eddy, a man who wants to be sedated?? You are the music and the music is you! You think I just picked my song off a jukebox? "I Don't Wanna Grow Up" was written by Tom Waits for the Bone Machine album, and he wrote that song for EXACTLY ME. It's about a young man, a few years into adulthood, looking at his parents, looking at his society, and stating firmly, "This is fucked, and I opt out." He doesn't want the car, or the mortgage, or the soul-sucking job, or to be bald and filled with doubt. He doesn't have an alternative solution, because he's running on fear, he's frantic, he's not thinking logically. The rhythm of it, the speed of the recording, the repetition – it's a tantrum. He's trying to stay a child, he's running as fast as he can in the opposite direction, even though there's NOTHING THERE. It's fucked up and it's inevitable. You can't not grow up. *(pause)* That's what Tom Waits knew. That's what the Ramones recorded. That's what I bring to the stage. Air guitar is hard work, The Nina. Here
(He smacks his head.)
and here
(He smacks his heart; almost angry)
You don't waltz into a qualifier with Journey because you're

mad at your ex-boyfriend. Some of us here want to win this because we believe it's special. You want to qualify in New York next month? You want to be an air guitar champion? You need to risk everything, because you're gonna have to take it over my dead body. I'm your friend at the bar, I'm your friend in the green room, but for those sixty seconds onstage, I'm your competition. And I bleed this.

For information on this author, click on the WRITERS tab at
www.smithandkraus.com

ALL ABOUT BIFFO
Stephen Bittrich

Comic
Sid, 40s

All about Biffo is a nod to the classic movie, All About
Eve. A young radical clown (Biffo) has challenged the
spotlight of a veteran clown (Sid). Sid has suffered a
painful burn on his rear end and is very angry with the
renegade, unprofessional Biffo.

SID

And that's another thing! Okay. While we're talking about
things... you are out of control! Thirty years I've been in this
business, ever since I was old enough to be shot out of a cannon, and not a single accident with the possible exception
of the leaky baby pool incident in '92. But that was a freak
accident! You, my friend, are reckless. You -- you come fresh
outta clown school one month to the day and already there
have been five -- count 'em -- five accidents, all of them in-
volving me. Not the least of which was second degree burns
on my back side! Oh yeah, sure, sure, laugh it up. It was your
job to run up with the spritzer bottle and put the fire out before it burns through the padding. I rely on you. Okay, you
couldn't find the spritzer bottle... fine! So you improvise. You
couldnt've grabbed the fire extinguisher? You couldnt've
grabbed the whipped cream pie? No, you had to grab a jug of
moonshine and splash it generously on my blazing backside.
Where did you even find a jug of moonshine!? What I want to
know is how highly flammable moonshine even got out there
in the first place?!

For information on this author, click on the WRITERS tab at
www.smithandkraus.com

ARCHIPELAGO
Caridad Svich

Dramatic
Ben, 20s-30s.

Ben is speaking to the audience, who throughout the play is his confidante. The love of his life – a woman named Hannah – has just left him.

BEN

The first time I lost her we were in the station I'd said the wrong thing, and she disappeared and left me standing with change in my pocket Ad little else. Spent the whole day in the station looking for her. Even slept there, thinking somehow maybe she'd come back. In the morning I walked out, miserable, angry, confused, not sure what had happened between us, except it was clear I'd said the wrong thing. And for all I knew she had gone to France and into another century to start a real fucking socialist revolution. This was May. Years before everything would start to turn and we'd find each other again, poised on the edge of another cliff, far away, wondering what had happened to us and if we were even meant to be together. She was older then, and memory had already started to play its tricks. As we watched whole cities burn. I wanted to say sorry for everything. Sorry for being a lousy traveler; sorry for being less than willing to see her at the other end. But I didn't say anything. When we found each other again, all I said was Hey, Hey. And I smiled and she smiled and there was that moment of wakefulness between us. And I forgot why I wanted to say sorry in the first place. All I could think of was, here we were on the cliff with another cliff before us and everything spinning too fast for our own good, while the shards of the world were nothing but desert.

ARCHIPELAGO
Caridad Svich

Dramatic
Ben, 20s-30s.

Ben is speaking to Hannah, the love of his life. They have been reunited, by chance, after many years of being apart. He has been in a hospital for a long time, and has only been out of it for about a year or so. He was shot by a sniper.

BEN

Your body. Missed it. Kept seeing your eyes. In dreams, memories, don't know, your eyes like the sun radiant and keeping the pulse of the entire world. Lying there, tubes fucked up bloated aching, weight of everything tears sadness cries in the halls, no one around, no one wanted to see me, after a while like dead I was, like a dead thing, on the slab oxygen melt brain fingers curled, look up at the sky, silence, blood, shame, thinking of you, wanting you, of all people, after years, why you… why…body goes numb, no words, a kind of beeping, that's what I… a beeping sound, body like a little drum, strange robot drum, like artifact from junk movie, junkyard robot man melting brain with a wink, it's what I did, wink, that was a word to them. Must be making progress. Must be coming out of coma. But in sleep I was eyes open listening everything everything, can't imagine the waste carbon footprint of hell waste all around, and the wheeling bed creaking down the hall a semblance of reality beep and loud prayers in the next room, people begging the gods for mercy quick now please, joke it was, joke to be there with bullet fucking ache, hurting like no words, eyes open everything everything I see but everyone like not there, like dead meat he is, not even worth prayer…sometimes gods would come, no name gods, not from a book, comic book gods, Superfuckingman, flying over the dead city of ruins like an angel of glorious vengeance, no flag, no allegiance except to good, do good in the world, make good, even when kindness is suspect, imagine that. Imagine kindness. Like flower, stone, rock in belly, arteries pumping strange liquid metal, blood metal lullabies singing a song of ancient rhyme and hopeful continents, no pasts to be buried, just kindness like flower spitting rain. And I, the dead thing, ghost one on the slab cot oxygen train dreaming a way out, wink, wink, words, he speaks, wink, he speaks again. Progress. Imagine progress in your hand blooming fire, letting go all that is critical care toxicology diagnosis he is awake. Think: Here. Picture. You. Think: miss your body. Like when we were full of feeling. Think: miss the city where I was ghost incarnate, not myself at all, but this other thing, this boy full of music and not a care and pretending we could drift through hours without anyone saying anything, because it was beautiful.

APROPOS OF NOTHING
Greg Kalleres

Comic
Owen, 30s-40s

Owen, slightly tispsy, takes the opportunity to chat it up with a stranger at a wedding reception, as his girlfriend dances off stage.

OWEN

Piccata. Right? It's always a piccata. At weddings? Veal, chicken, vegetable. I don't know even know what a piccata is but it's always there. I got the fish. It was good.

(Beat)

It's amazing how much time and energy is put into planning these things. The meal, the tastings -- well, you're married, you know. The tastings, the preparation, the *money,* right? And in the end, no one remembers because what you usually end up with is chicken piccata.

(beat)

Because the thing is, and I don't know you from Adam, I can tell you know what I'm talking about; sitting back here, alone, I can tell. The love, the ceremony, the *togetherness*, right? *All* of it. The affect on *us*, the *guests* -- I mean that's what it's all about. The *theater* of thing. And we all just pretend, you know? *(Before he can reply)* And *in* the relationship --! Sorry, I didn't mean to interrupt -- but *in* relationships, especially we pretend. Right? You pretend that you're as in love with her today as you were on the first day you fell in love. But it *fluctuates!* We know this. We like to think of love as this... line, this *hump* you get over, and once you've gotten over it, you're in love! Boom! And every day from then on is love. But this isn't true! We're not robots. You're in love one day and the next day you're not. You're on one side of the hump, and then you're on the other. Back and forth. Over and back. And why do we deny this?? *(Before he can reply)* Because the idea that love is fleeting -- is *terrifying!* "It feels so real one day, it *must* be real today!" But it isn't, so we pretend. Half of love is memory! Remembering what it felt like to love this person. She wants to have sex but you're not in the mood, it's clear you better get in the mood or this opportunity might not present itself again for a while. So what do you do? Have sex. Because you *remember!* "I remember that I'm in love with you. I remember what it feels like to *want* to have sex with you." Because eventually the pendulum will swing back around. *(Before he can reply)* And, hey, no, I believe in love! You know what true love is? When it's so real you *never* forget. Because every time you see her, you fall in love all over again. *(Beat)* Problem is -- the *truth?* There's someone else. And it's my best friend's wife, who I would never touch in a million years, but the truth is: I love her. True love. Martin has no idea and I would never tell him because what would that do? Plus they're "Martin & Lily" you know, it's like: "Martin & Lily!" It's an institution! You don't mess with that. I mean, they fall apart, this whole thing falls apart, let me tell you. Me, you, all of it. I tell you this because you seem like a man who understands. And sometimes...sometimes it feels good to say what's in your heart. You know? Sometimes you want to just say it, apropos of nothing. For once. No regard for what it means, the consequences and the like. Because sometimes you just need to feel like you still can!

For information on this author, click on the WRITERS tab at www.smithandkraus.com

THE ARSONISTS
Jacqueline Goldfinger

Dramatic
H, 50s

A father tries to convince his daughter to move on after hisdeath, and that there is no escaping certain fates.

H

You'd like tigers, Littles. Tigers always in flames. Stripes shimmer, Just with the walkin' of it. An' when it runs, Shit, Looks like fire spreadin' through the trees. From soil to sky, tall pines, row on row on row, with this streak of fire runnin' through it, leavin' nothin' behind. No smoke. No ashes. The cleanest burn you ever seen. A tiger's the best controlled burn. You'd be jealous ah that Littles. Even you with a hun'red packs ah matches couldn't do that. Burn so clean you leave nothin' behind. You can't be a tiger, all heat an' power an' control. You can't control the fire that good. Neither can I. Whether it be the fire or the heat or the police or the sheer weight of time There's always somethin' more than you, Littles. Somethin' out of your control. The wind kicks up. It kicks at the moment I light the head fuse. It catches my hand and wrist collar. Jump cross my arms, melts the buttons. At, when, at that, when it jumped, Cross my body. That's when I knew it. And I look across the field at you, Just, Doin', what I taught you, Just, shinin' in our own light. I knew you's ready. And I knew I's done. I said goodbye to you then, Littles. You couldn't get 'cross that field in-time unless you flew. And that's one I couldn't teach. What you can do now, Put me in the ground, give me peace. Leave. Start somethin' new. You can control that. You got a tiger by the tail, Doodlebug. You think you own it now, but that's a trick. It already owns you. You don't get out, it'll take what it wants in the end.

THE ARSONISTS
Jacqueline Goldfinger

Dramatic
H, 50s

A father tries to explain to his daughter why he loved her mother, even though the mother could be hurtful to the daughter.

H

Your mother and I, There was a time where I ... Before. I'd lived all my life in the heat. A child raised in fire. Living with, above, life. Skimming across the top. The unwaking world. There was the first time I saw her. ... But there was a space of time from when I took my first breath to when I really started breathing. That moment that usually lasts five seconds for ever'body else, Lasted 16 years for me. I mean, I knew how to get dressed and eat and sleep and lay fuses And diffuse the smell of gasoline. I did do the, the things you do. The waking life things. But it was mechanical. A machine of a boy, A machine of a man, Not breathing. Not living. There was a terrible completeness to it which in the back of my mechanical mind equaled life. A to B to C to D to E to F to end of day to end of night to end of morning to end of afternoon. The completeness we're told makes you full, makes life life. We'd weave and measure and cut and pretend to be the fates .But really, There was a coldness, Littles, A chill that just, froze inside me, kept me from really breathing. I'd stand in the warm afternoon rain not knowing why but craving the thaw. The first time I touched her hand, pretending it was an accident. Brushed my fingers over hers at the market, reaching for a grocery bag, I started gasping like a fish just reeled in on the boat. I dropped to my knees and thought I was going to die. Thought this is what it must feel like to be trapped in a blaze that won't ever turn over and burn out. Thought this is it. The cut. But she knelt down with me and took both my hands and we breathed together. And that was my first breath, Doodlebug, My honest to God first. And when we rose up together, I was a new man. I was 16 and just born and that was it. I think you've been born, Littles, but you don't breathe. You don't live like how your Momma did for me. You haven't started breathing yet.

THE ART OF THE FUGUE
Don Nigro

Dramatic
Andrew, 22

*In the summer of 1920, Andrew Rose and his older
brother Jamie are back from serving in the Army in
France in World War I, and both are troubled and
traumatized young men. Their father, a teacher, has
just committed suicide, tormented with guilt for im-
pregnating one of his students. Their sister Jane, an
accomplished violinist, has just graduated from the
Conservatory of Music and has brought her best
friend Felicia home with her, to their family house in
a small town in east Ohio, to spend the summer pre-
paring for their first concert tour of Europe in the fall.
Felicia is a brilliant and very beautiful pianist with
emotional problems and a dark family history, and is
having a rather good time watching Jamie fall hope-
lessly in love with her, while Andrew tries to seduce
her. Jamie has been the leader of two large families of
siblings and cousins all through their childhood, and
is loved and respected by everyone but Andrew, who
has always been desperately jealous of his brother,
and whose horrible experiences in the war have only
increased the intensity of his hatred. Andrew has apparently been successful with Felicia, and it's tearing
Jamie apart. Jamie is also concerned that Andrew
will do serious harm to her, and has just warned him
to leave her alone. This is Andrew's response. He is
gloating, goading his brother, and very much enjoying
defeating and humiliating him.*

ANDREW

I should leave her alone, or what? Or you're going to what? Give me a good, sound thrashing if I don't? Really? Do you think that would impress her? Because I don't think so. Although it's true some women are excited by violence, and she might well be one of them, but, trust me, nothing you can do will impress her enough to make her want you. I'm the one she's drawn to. All these pretty girls, these prim, well brought up girls are like that. They're drawn to bad behavior, like the preacher's daughter. They're excited by cruelty. They confuse it with strength. They want to do it in cheap, dirty rooms in cheap, dirty hotels. Or under the piano. Which is surprisingly nice, by the way. I've been listening to you my whole life, especially when you weren't saying anything, which was most of the time. You can't stand for once not being the chosen one, can you? You can't stand it that for once I get something and not you. All your life, it's been you, and not me. People like you. They don't like me. People feel safe with you. They feel uneasy with me. They want to tell you their troubles. They don't want to tell me anything. But she wants me. Not you. Me. She wants me. And you can't deal with it. It's lovely. I've never been happier. You could kill me right now and I'd die a happy man, and she still wouldn't want to sleep with you. And you do want to kill me, don't you? You've always wanted to kill me. Well, take your best shot, brother. You can borrow my service revolver if you like. But just a friendly word of advice: Don't miss.

THE ART OF THE FUGUE
Don Nigro

Dramatic
Andrew, 25

It's 1923 in a hotel room somewhere in Europe, and Andrew Rose and his older brother Jamie have been touring for three years with their sister Jane, a violinist, and her beautiful and brilliant but increasingly unbalanced friend Felicia, a pianist, the center piece of whose program is Bach's The Art Of The Fugue, *which she practices obsessively and which is slowly helping to drive her insane. Felicia has a dark history of family abuse, and she has chosen as her lover Andrew, who is cruel to her, over Jamie, who loves her deeply and tries to protect her. Andrew manages the tour, while Jamie, the older brother Andrew has always resented, is reduced to making sure their luggage gets on the train and tuning the piano. Andrew has been greatly enjoying his triumph over his brother, but listening to Felicia play the Bach fugues over and over again has been getting on his nerves. Jamie has just come upon him being violent with Felicia, and tells him "If you ever hurt her again—" but doesn't finish the sentence. This is Andrew's response.*

ANDREW

If I ever hurt her again, what? Speak up. I can't hear you. What a pathetic sight you are. You're ridiculous. The piano tuning stage door Johnny to a depraved lunatic. She pities you. When I was about twelve, I heard a noise in the middle of the night, and I looked out the window, and there was our father, sitting on the porch, at three in the morning, just sobbing like a baby. Over that poor, stupid girl, I'm sure. And I told myself, I will never be like that. Not me. I'm going to make THEM cry. But you're just like him. And you're going to end up the same way, too. What a damned couple of fools. God, my head hurts. Do you hear that? I keep hearing something like insects buzzing. Maybe they're insects. Maybe they're aliens. Actually, it's probably those god damned fugues. I can't get the fucking things out of my head. I hate those fugues almost as much as I hate you. I used to stay up late, waiting for you to come home. I was hoping you'd be killed on the road, or in some drunken brawl, or with your pants down at the whore house. Something humiliating like that. She's mine. Not yours. Mine. To take possession. That's the only truth. The only reality. To take possession. And she's all mine. So, are you going to try and kill me, or what?

BLOOD AT THE ROOT
Dominique Morisseau

Dramatic
Colin, late teens, African-American

The students at Colin's high school have staged a demonstration protesting a racist act, which Colin has found inspiring.

COLIN

It was like some shit out of a Civil Rights documentary. Like the kind they be showin' in class. And most of the folks be fallin' half asleep. Seen this one kid in 3rd period start droolin' on the desk when we was watchin' this one---Eyes on the Prize it called. Real interestin' to me, but guessin' not to most everbody else. I interested cuz it's nice to know what done happened before I showed up somewhere. Nice to know how thangs used to be and that thangs as they is now come from somethin'. It all got roots. Way somebody choose not to sit next to somebody in the lunchroom-got roots. Way somebody got problems with the flag somebody else wear on they t-shirt - got roots. Way some people talk the way they talk, or hang out with who they hang out with, or love who they love, or hate who they hate - all got roots. It feel halfway comfortin' knowin' it ain't just start with us. That it been this way. That somebody's been plantin' these awful feelins in the soil somewhere. Long before we came along and started pulling up crops. We been digestin'
this same stuff, grown in this same soil, and ain't even know it. So I like seein' stuff like that... Eyes on the Prize... documentaries on the Civil Rights Movement. When that happened today at school...when those students went and stood under that great oak tree... Ol' Devoted they call it.... Look like some kinda protest. Look like somethin' like from another time.

From a Civil Rights Time. And it got me thinkin'…what kinda crop is the folks after us gonna dig up? Is it still gonna be from this same ol' soil? Or is we ever gonna plant somethin' new?

For information on this author, click on the WRITERS tab at www.smithandkraus.com

BLOOD AT THE ROOT
Dominique Morisseau

Dramatic
Justin, late teens, African-American

Some white kids have pulled a racist prank at Justin's high school, and the black kids have staged a demonstration protesting it. Here, Justin explains why he won't take sides.

JUSTIN

Things at Cedar High can be real divided. Lots of lines get drawn and everybody wanna know what side you standin' on. Now me? I get by like I always done. Be studious. Be focused. Be attentive. That's never done me much for popularity. Doesn't give me the most friends. Keeps me... well... I don't like Toria callin' it invisible. I mean what does she... who does she... she doesn't know me. Nobody knows me. That's the point. But at this stage in the game, I'm not askin' for that anymore. Sure, it might've bothered me when I was a kid. What kid likes to be the outcast? Sure, it might've made me sad or like some story from a after school special. But that's not the case anymore. I figured out that none of that matters anymore. Folks like me ... there's no space where we really fit, y'know? No side we really make sense on. I've always just existed in the cracks. So when they come askin' me where I stand, what do I say? Whose side am I supposed to take? Black kids protestin'. White kids prankin'. What side am I supposed to be on when don't none of them ever ... when ain't none of 'em really ... when I just seem to belong to myself. And that's it. That's the side I'm on. But here at Cedar High, everybody want you on a side. Wanna know where your loyalties lie. And what I got to say about it? Who's been loyal to me? Find me one person that can answer that question, and I'll tell you what side I'm on. Til' then, it's all about bein' objective. That's the only way I know to survive. In the cracks.

For information on this author, click on the WRITERS tab at www.smithandkraus.com

BOYS NIGHT
Gary Richards

Comic
Frank, 50

Frank is talking to a friend on a Soho, New York, roof-top.

FRANK

So, check it out, I'm out in L.A. and I'm paying through the nose for a dumpy, rinky-dink hotel room that has the nerve to charge for porn, so I had to get out. I lace up my running shoes and take a run along the boardwalk from Santa Monica to Venice to scope out the local talent, and I see all these homeless guys and I think, "Wow, what a great place to be homeless!" Right? I mean, if you're going to be homeless in America, it's a great option. The weather is great every day, you're on the beach every day, you're gawking at babes in bathing suits every day. You wake up, maybe take a morning dip. Reach into the garbage for yesterday's newspaper, a couple of cold fries. And you could probably scrounge enough money to sip on a Mai Tai every now and then. Right? Clifford, the homeless guy that lives on my block, I'm betting he's not sipping Mai Tais and smelling cocoa butter. Never. And forget body surfing. I guarantee Clifford hasn't body surfed in quite some time. So I see Clifford the other day picking a butt off the ground and I ask him where he was originally from. He tells me Indiana. So I ask Clifford why the fuck he picked New York City to be homeless in. You know what he tells me? "The diversity!" You fucking believe that?! "The diversity!" He says, "Where else can I meet homeless people from all over the world?" Clifford could be on a beach in Santa Monica, soaking up the rays, smelling the cocoa butter, and playing fucking beach volleyball!! But he wants diversity! Instead he's squatting on a bench at the corner in front of Crate and Barrel saving all his nickels and dimes so he can suck down another Jamba Juice.

For information on this author, click on the WRITERS tab at www.smithandkraus.com

BLUE/WHITNEY
Steven Haworth

Seriocomic
Virgil, 16, African-American

*Virgil's fifteen-year old white girlfriend ran away from
her home in Westchester and was murdered, Virgil
is accused, but Whitney's mother is convinced of his
innocence and bails him out of jail so he can give her
a tour of the life her daughter lived before she died.
Here Virgil tells the story of how he met Whitney, who
he knew as Blue.*

VIRGIL

Check it out. I'm on the One train. Back in May. Goin' downtown. Morning rush hour. Some train went out a service so
Number One is packed *tight*. All the suits is *miserable*. I say
suits 'cause when I say downtown I mean everybody going to
Wall Street. We pull into Franklin Street station. Doors stop in
front a this white dude. Pinstripe suit. Gold watch. Briefcase.
Like in his thirties. He is like *aaarrrgh!* He *need* to get on that
train! Nobody gets off. No *way* nobody gettin' on. He ain't just
put out. He is like a straight up exploding brain! He *got* to get
to Wall Street or his life is over! So what does he do? Reaches
out. Pulls a young lady *off* the train. Gets in her spot. This shorty
little white rabbit on her way to Wall Street. Yellow blouse. Pearls
around her neck. Short blonde hair tucked around big ears with a
little pink nose. Little White Rabbit standing on the platform. She
can't believe it. People on the train they can't believe it. Doors
jerkin' tryin' to close. Pinstripe Dude holding his briefcase to his
chest. Squeezin' his eyes shut please God let the doors close!
Then I see. Right there. This pretty little white girl with blue
hair. Now who is this white girl with blue hair, Mrs. Wing?
That's right, it's Blue, Mrs. Wing. But I ain't know her yet so

I'm a call her Blue-headed White Girl. Blueheaded White Girl got her hands on the door and won't let it close! Pinstripe Dude lookin' at her like "What you doin', bitch!" But she won't let the doors close. So the doors open up again. What does she do?! SHE TRIES TO PUSH HIM OFF THE TRAIN! She tryin' to push this Pinstripe Motherfucker right out the door! I am like damn! But she can't budge him. He like twice her size. So I say to myself "V?! THIS A MOMENT A TRUTH, NIG-GA! You gonna let this little white girl lose this battle?! Lose this battle against Pinstripe Muthafucka Tyrannical Bullshit?! And do you know what the answer was, Mrs Wing? The answer was NO! Hell no! I take Pinstripe Motherfucker up by the collar! I throw that Pinstripe Motherfucker off the train! I'm like "Get off the train, Pinstripe Motherfucker!" I grab little White Rabbit, pull her back on the train. Point at Pinstripe Motherfucker, I'm like "Stay there, motherfuc-ker." Blue-headed White Girl is like "Yeah, motherfucker!" So there's Pinstripe Motherfucker. Standing on the platform. Mouth hangin' open. Soul gone. Cryin' like a bitch! Blue-headed White Girl lets go the door. Train start to move. And the whole subway car – BURSTS INTO APPLAUSE! I look at my new friend. I say, "Hey! I'm V!" She's like: "I'm Blue." I say, "Really? 'Cause you look happy." She's like: "No, 'cause a my hair, stupid." I'm like, "I know I'm just playin'." She's like, "Oh okay." And that's how I met Blue!

For information on this author, click on the WRITERS tab at www.smithandkraus.com.

BREACH
Barret O'Brien

Comic
Young Man, 27

Four strangers have taken refuge from the rising waters of a once-a-century flood in a dive bar at the edge of the French Quarter, New Orleans. Here the Young Man tries to lift the flagging spirits of the others.

YOUNG MAN

So...pops, psycho, and I are walking down Decatur Street one night and the devil pops up out of the sidewalk. Poof! And he says, "Y'all want to see hell?" And I'm all, "Hells yeah." So we all go down on this big ole escalator and there are these clocks everywhere...on the walls. *Everywhere.* Well, pops, being the keen observer that we now know he is, says, "What's wit' all the clocks?" And el diablo says, he says, "Well these map people's masturbation habits. Every time one of you rubs one out the minute hand moves one notch. You make it clear across the face of your clock, I know I'm doin' A-okay on the temptation front." Then the devil points out one on the far wall which reads four-thirty. "Right there, pops. That's yours." Not bad for an old-timer we all think. So psycho asks, "Where's mine?" And the devil points one out, "Right there." Psycho's reads two-seventeen. So I pipe in, ever the eager, "And mine? Where mine at?" And the devil looks me straight in the eye and, without even cracking a smile, son-of-a-gun says, "Yours? Oh, I keep yours in my office. Got it above my desk. Use it as a ceiling fan." (*no reactions*) It's funnier in Spanish.

THE CHANGING ROOM
Joseph Krawczyk

Comic
Frank, 46-55

At his wife's urging, Frank has walked into the changing room of a Gap clothing store to try on a new pair of jeans. Unable to exit the changing room, he finds himself trapped in an alternate dimension.

FRANK

I don't understand. I walked into The Gap with my wife Stella and entered the changing room to try on a new pair of jeans. And then poof, I stumbled into something, somewhere and I'm trapped into what I can only guess is another dimension. Not sure where I am now at this point or how I got into this echoless chamber. Hey, this is different. Did someone turn the lights out? Hello, is anyone out there? Where the hell am I? It's dark and cold in here. And I feel as if I'm hurtling through space at warp speed. Where's that damn Mr. Spock when you need him? What's going on? What's happening to me? Somebody, anybody, get me out of here…Oh, damn, I'm panicking. Stay calm, Frank, stay calm. Take deep breaths. C'mon you can do this. You'll figure something out. Hey, can anyone hear me? Why am I in this place, trapped in what feels like some kind of spongy membrane? What's the story here? Did I fall through a trap door? Did I get consumed by a whale? Stella, are you out there? Can you hear me? I think I died and stumbled into hell, because this is definitely not heaven. I'm all alone and I don't know what to do or how to get back to you. I love you and I miss you. Am I in a rabbit hole like *Alice in Wonderland*? Is that what I've fallen into? Yes, a rabbit hole, but there are no rabbits. Where the hell are the rabbits? Or, at least, tell me where I can find the rabbits. Is it something I've done? Is that why I'm here? I'm being punished, but for what? What did I do to deserve this? I've always been faithful to you, Stella, I swear. Well, there was that one time with your sister, but it didn't mean anything. There's got to be an exit somewhere around here. But all I feel are walls. Even the characters in Sartre's *No Exit* had a chance to leave if they wanted to. Can anyone hear me?! Hello-o-o-o-o-o-o-o-o-o. This place just goes on forever. It's infinite. A labyrinth. Like I'm in some kind of parallel universe but there are no stars, no moon, just this incredible twilight. How long will I have to be in here? Stella, I'm trapped in some kind of bubble and I can't find a way out. Wait a minute, I know… Why didn't I think of this before? Where's my phone? I'll just call 911. Damn, the battery's dead. I've got to get out of here. We've got expensive tickets for *Hamilton* tonight! Six hundred dollars each, and they're not refundable. What am I gonna' do now?!

(He falls to the floor and screams at the top of his lungs for his wife Stella and tears at his shirt like Stanley Kowalski from A Streetcar Named Desire.*)*
STELLA!!!

CHASING THE STORM
Sandra A. Daley-Sharif

Dramatic
Abioh: 30s, Any Race

The group realizes that Aquah is right. Abioh is a traitor. He works for the Bureau. He defends his actions.

ABIOH

You can trust me. I swear to you. I would've killed you already, if that's what I aim to do. I could've turned you all in. I'm a Drop-Out. Just like you. That's the truth. I was helping to mobilize cities... New York, Boston... That's what I do. Long before I was called in to organize Ocean City, I was building pools, dragging water from nearby springs. Helping to equalize, because there was anarchy, those who had means had seized dozens of natural springs, limiting access to already scarce water supply. These past, what 40 years, globally, we've been brought to our knees... We're in a wasteland... living in a desert. No water. Desolate....To stand on lines for the basic necessities. How is that possible? In America? All this technology and we can't make enough clean water to survive... What you don't know is, they started killing Devlins. The Bureau. The Bureau of Counterterrorism. Said there were people stealing from the water supply. They didn't have a name for them at first. Until they noticed that these people were different and there were more of them "cropping" up. Said that they were underground varmints, using what they called "their gift" for their own benefit. Devlins. There's an enforcement team responsible for rounding them up, going into their homes in the middle of the night, stealing them from their beds, their families, and locking them up. Killing them. You won't get far. You'll be slaughtered. Is that what you want? It's top intelligence. Contrary to the mandates going out to the public. They are telling us it's the rainfall, that we're collecting. If it *is* some underground source, some natural spring, or pool, plenty of it, and rich with resources, you won't get close. CT won't let you. They will kill for a lot less. Will use water for leverage, as a weapon, and to suppress naysayers. Two years ago when that small town, Spicewood was under attack, their camps weren't quite organized, CT spared no expense to protect the water infrastructure. Well, I tell you... If it's as hidden as you say... this pool. They are not apt to share it with the likes of us. Only a privileged few know about it, I'm sure, and are living there. Like you said. It is the old 1%. Get close, and they will round you up and kill you. I've seen it. One night, they dragged a family back from the desert. A mother, father, and their two young boys. Both no more than 8 years old. Said they couldn't have these *varmints* wandering off. Locked them all up in a iron cell. CT questioned them for days. Fed them next to nothing. And drops of water. And finally, the devlin, they tortured her. They slaughtered her in front of her family. Probed her every senses. Immersed her in a frigid black pool. Peeled away her skin, looking for sensors. Looking for mutated cells in her hands. In her feet. They hooked her like a fish.

CONTENT NO MORE
Steve Koppman

Comic
Gene, 20s

Mike, a middle-aged industry analyst for The Wisdom Group ('We know the answer! What's the question?'), is in a first-time in-person meeting with his boss, 20-something Gene, who expresses 'concerns' about 'throwback' Mike's work and enlightens him on the goals of the company's new Director of Thought, ('Our number one goals in 2019 are to be the source of all insight' and 'to be part of every decision anyone makes') further embodied in Wisdom's new Enlightenment product suite, whose introduction Gene explains to Mike.

GENE

If I believed anyone was doing anything to besmirch the name of Wisdom, I'd stop it in a heartbeat. What I see are hundreds of the world's finest analysts working to the best of their abilities within constraints of time. You want to know what's really going on? We've asked customers what they want. So we know, Mike! I talk to 'em every day. You know what they care about? Nothing like you say. They're united on one thing. They don't want to waste time reading! Their time's too valuable for Mickey Mouse crap like that. What they demand is more and more and more inside less and less and less. In 2018 we're giving it to 'em. More and more impactful, actionable thought in smaller and smaller and smaller bites! That's why our Enlightenment product will come down next month from many pages to: one. We're not stopping there! That page will come down in third quarter to a paragraph. Any page can be summed up in a paragraph. Then, in the fourth quarter, a sentence. Then, in 19 -- what do we need a whole sentence? Sum it in a key word. Then, maybe a syllable. Finally a letter! Shorter the better! By the end of 19, our research will be something you take with lunch, in a cup of coffee, a glass of water. Yes, no, OK, a shrug, a nod, a snort, a sigh, maybe just a weary knowing silence. They'd much rather have that than all your verbiage! What our customers want's easy access and not to waste time reading like a bunch of nerds! But it's what we need too, Mike. 'Cause Wisdom can charge more and more and more for less and less and less!

CRY IT OUT
Molly Smith Metzler

Dramatic
Mitchell, late 30s-early 40s

*Mitchell is very dismayed that his wife seems to lack
interest in their newborn daughter. He is talking to a
neighbor, Jessie, who has adjusted well to being a new
mother. He doesn't know what to do.*

MITCHELL

I have not seen her *touch* our daughter in five and a half
weeks. The hardest thing is that I really can't gauge how much
of this has to do with her work and how much doesn't. Or maybe it was moving out here? I don't know. It's been a big change.
(But we built her a studio in the basement? -- I thought she'd
be thrilled.) And the doctor said it could certainly be all the
IVF we did-- failed IVF can take a psychological toll on the
mother. But I don't think that's what it is -- Adrienne was *happy* when she was pregnant. She threw up *every day*, and still
she was in good humor. We were just so grateful to finally be
pregnant. And she designed the nursery in the new house, in
this beautiful giraffe theme? But I don't think she's been in
that room since. Like an alien stole my wife. And I'm trying
to be understanding because she's under a lot of professional
pressure right now, I know that. She landed a big account at
work just before we had Livia-- which should be exciting but
the whole thing has just made her manic. And she doesn't *need*
to be manic; she has a staff in Brooklyn who can handle everything while she's on leave, she's *supposed to be on leave*. But
she's locking herself in her studio for days at a time, working
on some ear cuff a celebrity wants made for red carpet season
or some custom ring for some PR person's wedding. (She's a
jewelry designer, that's what she does). And I keep saying *let*

your team handle this, Adrienne, that's what they're for. You *have a seven week old and you are missing her -- you wanted her and you're missing her--* and she just slams her studio door and says that if I loved her I'd understand. And maybe that's true? I don't know. I have nothing to compare any of this to. But she forgets to come upstairs and she forgets to eat and she forgets to sleep and she forgets to take Livie to *the one fucking Mommy & Me class* she's supposed to take her to.....I think she forgets we had Livie.

For information on this author, click on the WRITERS tab at
www.smithandkraus.com

DEAD WOMAN'S GAME
Erik Christian Hanson

Seriocomic
Jimmy, 28

Jimmy, 28, an unemployed chatterbox, tries to rescue Ren, his suicidal friend, from the clutches of a psych ward.

JIMMY

Had a dream last night that the President of the United States made various forms of technology illegal on account of the fact that it was making people dumber. Ruder. Blackberrys, IPods, IPads, I-whatever-the-fuck those computer geeks in Seattle-have created, all of it, illegal. Beauty of the President's decision was that it actually made people talk to each other. Look at each other. Listen to each other. Did wonders for domestic peace. I wanted the dream to go on forever. I wanted the dream to become *my* reality. But I woke up in an alley, looked around and there were cell phones and I-things there, there, everyfucking- where around me. And nobody was talking to each other. Nobody was looking at each other. Nobody was listening to each other. *(Pause)* People believe they're communicating and it's healthy, but it's not. It shuts more people out than it lets in. Life should be about inclusion, not exclusion. The people are sheep. Programmed. The commercial asks them, "You need the latest and greatest Blackberry?" If you do, it's on sale now. Only now. A one-day sale. Rush out and get one before it's too late. And the people buy the latest and greatest Blackberry. Unfortunately for them, somebody creates a newer version a week later. The 7.1. Blackberry. Last week's version, the one they just purchased, has been made extinct. So they take the one they bought last week, turn it in for credit so they can get the new one, the 7.1. Start using it.

Post the fact that they got the 7.1 on their Twitter account or Facebook account. "Got the 7.1 Blackberry! Oh, yes, I did. Aren't I cool? How do you like me now?" And everybody likes them now. But the comedy never stops because an hour later, a friend posts, "I got the 7.2 Blackberry. Here are pictures of me with it. Don't we look cute together?" *(Pause)* No more privacy. Everything is public. How do you think I found out about you?

DISTRICT MERCHANTS
Aaron Posner

Dramatic
Antoine DuPre, 50s-60s, African-American

Antoine Du Pre is a wealthy and successful African-American merchant who made his money in... complicated ways, during the Civil War. He is now a solid citizen and leader in his community, trying to do the best he can for himself and his people in trying times. He is speaking to the audience. He wants us to understand.

ANTOINE

What do you see when you look at me? What assumptions do you make? What will I have to work against? Those questions are like breathing to me. That... *commonplace.* Because folks don't know exactly what to make of me, don't know what box I fit in. "Just *what kind of black man is this?"* they wonder. I see it every day. You see... I was born a free man. A free child, in a world of bondage. My father was... pressed into the Navy during the war of 1812. He won his freedom through "exemplary service to the nation." *Exemplary Service.* And then was shot dead on New Year's Day, 1823, because a white man thought he'd looked at his daughter wrong. I was five. My sister Bess was three. My sister Grace was born about three weeks after the funeral. I remember his smell. Soap ... salt... And a rumbly voice. And that's about all...My mother was... careful. Not kind. Not cruel. *Careful.* She always told me "Look behind" That was her... *daily admonition.* Her only philosophy. I'd say "His mama so mean" and she'd say *"Look behind.* That boy Sassy, she got to keep him safe." Or I'd say... those white folks is so this or so that, and she's say *"Look behind all that.* See their fear. See the danger." I was raised up always "looking behind"... trying to see what was really going on... A valuable skill, as it turns out, for a black man in America.

For information on this author, click on the WRITERS tab at www.smithandkraus.com

DISTRICT MERCHANTS
Aaron Posner

Seriocomic
Ben, 20s-30s, African-American

Benjamin Bassanio has just asked his mentor, Antoine Du Pre, for funds to help woo a wealthy young woman. Benjamin is a very light-skinned black man, light enough to pass, and did not tell Antoine that the woman he is wooing is white.

BEN

I just lied and lied and lied and lied... but I never told a single lie. Every word was true. Except there were also the words I *didn't* say, words like... "She's white." And "When in Belmont, *so am I...*" I feel bad lying to him, but he'd never understand. He'd see her color, and my *betrayal*, and that's it. But I... I won't just stay a part of the damn problem: Another uppity Negro with nowhere to climb up to. *This country.* This country is built to drive us all insane. Or people like me, anyway... But, no, seriously, here's how it goes: America sidles up to you in her pretty red dress and says, Hey handsome, here's everything you could ever want, right here for the taking. So you say, Well, great, can I have some of it? And she says, Absolutely! So you say, How? And she says Just Step Right Up, so you say, Ummm, how do I do that? And she says "YOU CAN'T!" So you say... But you just said I could. And she says, And you can...! And so you say, But how? And she says, Just Come and Get It! So you say, Really??? And she says, "NO, NOT REALLY!!!" So, after a while you *try something*. And America knocks you on your trusting black ass and says, Nope, not that way. So you try something else. Same thing happens. And again. And again. And *again* and *again* and *again*... And you know why? Oh, wait, hold up...

you do know why, don't you? People like me—we don't know the code. Any of the codes... And we don't have the key. *Any of the keys*...We don't even know the rules, and we don't even know which rules we don't even know! But here's the thing. My father knew the codes. He knew the rules, he had the keys, and he also owned my mother and me. That's right: My father *literally* owned me. And now suppose that this raping, swaggering, devoutly Christian father is actually often *kind*. Helpful, even. He taught me to read. And some of the codes, and some of the rules... and then he died. And at thirteen I was suddenly "free." In America. "The land of opportunity." And I *know* some things. And I *want* some things. And I've been knocked on my ass time after time by—excuse my language—ignorant shit-heads... and to be honest, I'm tired of it.

For information on this author, click on the WRITERS tab at www.smithandkraus.com

THE DOG IN THE DRESSING ROOM
Deborah Savadge

Seriocomic
Joel, 30s

Joel is the company manager of a play in rehearsals. He has been beating around the bush about his romantic interest in Kira, the leading lady. Here, he declares the way he feels about her.

JOEL

I saw you come in and I thought, "She's beautiful. I think she's the most …radiantly …beautiful woman I've ever stood near." And then we were introduced and you smiled at me and said my name and "Hello" and "Happy to meet you," and I thought, "I love her voice. Maybe a little Emma Stone mixed with a bit of Laura Linney and a dash of early Nicole Kidman." And then you got up onstage and you took a moment to prepare. "An Actor Prepares."
(He laughs.)
And I could see you were intelligent and and an artist. And I thought "God! I love actors." …And then you read, and it was simple, and truthful and you did that thing with your arm, (He throws his arm out and reels it in, in imitation of her. It's funny and accurate.) And I thought, "She's breathtaking."…And with that thought, I felt dizzy. Like I couldn't get my breath. And a voice in my head said, "I want that in my life. That that that fineness."…And then you got down off the stage and you talked to Rob and Holly about schedule conflicts and I watched you. And I could see you wanted the role more than anything. And Rob shook your hand. It was clear he was enthusiastic. And you thanked him and covered his hand with your other hand.

(He extends his arm and covers his right hand with his left.)

And you thanked Holly and touched her arm. And she looked grateful. She was smiling.

(He imitates a broad grin.)

Which is pretty unusual for Holly. And when you walked up the aisle you saw me. And you could tell I was rooting for you to get it and you did a little,

(He does a little mini-victory dance.)

And then you kind of shrugged. And I was… a goner.

For information on this author, click on the WRITERS tab at www.smithandkraus.com

THE DOG IN THE DRESSING ROOM
Deborah Savadge

Dramatic
Joel, 30s

*Joel is the company manager for a play in rehearsal.
He is smitten with Kira, the leading lady, but she has
reservations about his past. Here, he comes clean.*

JOEL

I'm sorry. I know you didn't want me back here tonight, but
I've been walking around and around and around, thinking
about everything that was said, and everything that was Not
said and I just felt I had to come back here and tell you – try
to – tell you - why you have to give me a second chance –
third chance probably… fourth chance. Why you have to hear
me out because – I understand you don't believe this yet, but
you and I are meant to be together. So we can't let something
I screwed up get in the way of that because, because...Let me
just explain. *(Deep breath.)* Victoria and I were very young
when we met and it was a very uncomplicated relationship at
first – for a long time. We studied together and hung out and it
was a very easy…we had fun. It wasn't a great passion or anything, but we had good times together and then, when she went
to graduate school, she fell madly in love with a professor, her
advisor, and he was married, and she thought he would leave
his wife and his three kids for her – even though everyone was
telling her: that wasn't very likely – but she broke it off with
me because she was so sure that this was going to to to happen.
And then she found out she wasn't the first or the second - or
even the third - of his advisees to to to – that he – put the moves
on – and then, when she realized she was just one in a series

---

– even though he still insisted that this was Different and that he was going to leave his wife, but she was broken-hearted and she…she came to me and and asked for my forgiveness and wanted to get back together, and so we did. And then she wanted to get married and and so we did – even though we both had – I really think we both had a sinking feeling that this wouldn't – that it was a bad idea. But then we had only been married for a matter of of of weeks, really, when the professor left his wife and kids after all and and, at first, Victoria just took the position that it was too late; that she was married to Someone Else...Me. And she wouldn't see him, but he he stalked her. He followed her. He stalked *us*. He called in the middle of the night. He would show up at our door. And finally he just – wore her down. Or rather this great Passion was no match for our little companionable, reasonably happy, but not not not…Anyway, she left me - for him - and we got a divorce. We started to pursue an annulment, at first, but that seemed to deny that we…and anyway, that's more of a Catholic thing, and neither of us is…. So we we got a divorce and because he has money - He's kind of a famous scholar in his field, so they have a yard for for for Molly. And I didn't, at the time, even have an apartment. So they got, as you said, "custody" of Molly and I would get – bones and chew toys for her, sometimes. And this went on for a while and I was, I was over it. And then I saw you at the audition and I knew. I finally knew what it was like to be to be knocked out, totally and completely struck by by by… Love. By the need, the longing, to do whatever it would take to be with this person – You. For for for always …

For information on this author, click on the WRITERS tab at www.smithandkraus.com

DOORMEN
Penny Jackson

Dramatic
Phil, 40-50

Twenty-five years later, the simmering hatred from the victims of the Bosnian war are ignited when a middle-aged Serbian man, Phil, is hired as a doorman in an Upper West Side building where all the other doormen, particularly Milo, are Bosnian refugees who hate Serbs. Two teenagers in the building, Josh and Lydia, become involved in the feud. Here Phil, the Serbian doorman, warns Lydia to stay away.

PHIL

You like Milo. You're protecting him. I understand. But what does Serb mean to you anyway? What does a young American girl know about war? You ever see anyone shot in the head, Lydia? Brains spilling out of their scalps? Eyes gouged out of the sockets from torture? Do you know what a real battle is? Not something you watch in your Star Wars movies. My people were guilty. So were the Bosnians. No nice people when you're at war. This is the stuff they don't show on The History Channel. Soldiers using axes to hack the babies right out of their mothers' bellies. Making the grandfathers shoot their own grandsons. What those soldiers did to women - sickening. Didn't matter how old they were. Eight or eighty. Didn't matter. Those men couldn't see what they were doing. Or hear. Or feel. That's what happens in war. Makes you deaf, dumb and blind. Inhuman. You don't need to know these things. Lydia, so leave it alone. Leave it alone. Do what you like to do - make out with your boyfriend, smoke pot, dance in clubs. Because you're lucky. You were born in the right country in the right time with the right religion and the right face and the right place. Every night you should fall to your knees and pray to God for your good fortune. Me? I can't do that. History has played its practical joke and landed me in a job surrounded by my enemies.

DUSTING FOR VOMIT
Neal Reynolds

Comic
Gary, late-20s to late-40s

Gary, a star actor, tries to pitch another star on a movie script with great roles for both of them, which will only get made if they both do it.

GARY

The movie is going to be called "Dusting for Vomit." Or maybe "Dusting for Vomit -- a CSI Movie." Or maybe "CSI colon..." I'm not kidding. It's inspired by the unsolved murder of a British rock band drummer back in the sixties. He choked to death on vomit. Somebody else's vomit. Remember, back then there was no way for the police to figure out whose vomit it was. As one of the band members put it, "you can't dust for vomit." With modern DNA forensics techniques, now you *can* "dust for vomit!" All you have to do is get a sample of DNA from each suspect and see which one matches the DNA of the fatal vomit! A CSI investigator doesn't have to go around to all the suspects and get them to vomit into a specimen bag! A cotton swab from the inside of a person's mouth has enough DNA in it. You of all people should know that, Bill. (Pause) Okay, okay. I'm sorry. I know you're trying to put those days behind you and get back to the stage. But I really need you, Bill. The studio financial guys said that they will only put up the money if we're both in it! They plan to promote the movie as "a battle between the titans of crime scene investigation!" You get to play the murderer! The guy who throws up in the drummer's mouth! Don't you just love it! Bill? Where you going? Should I have my agent call yours to set up the deal?

EL NOGALAR
Tanya Saracho

Dramatic
Lopez, 30s

Memo Lopez was once a humble worker in the estate's pecan orchard, but is now a successful entrepreneur, mainly due to his ability to stay under the radar and play all sides of a quarrel. Here he explains to Dunia, the housekeeper, that things aren't the way they used to be with the growing influence of the The Maña (the local cartel) and that it's better for people like them to keep their mouths shut and know their place.

LOPEZ

You know why I end up worrying about other people's shit? Because people don't know when to shut the fuck up around here, that's why. If I have nothing to say, I don't open my mouth. That has been my greatest gift. Zip it. Laugh when everyone else is laughing, even if you don't understand the joke, laugh anyway. And then shut your mouth. Nowadays if someone sees you open your mouth, even to take a breath, a black truck with tinted windows will come driving down the road and carry you off to the most unfortunate corners of the hills. So everybody should just shut their mouths. Half the shit people say is stupid anyway. Half the shit that people write too. People and their words. Words are for idle people. People who don't have to earn a living. *(beat)* This was the last room I got to see inside this house... we were never allowed upstairs. Well, the playroom, we were only allowed inside the playroom if we were bringing things up or moving furniture, but never the master bedroom. I always thought this room would be bigger, with draperies everywhere and maybe with gold things on the walls or something. But when I finally made it upstairs and came in to see it... *(beat)* You always think things are better on the other side when the door is closed on you. You imagine it in your head with more color or something. Like this bed. Everyone talked about this bed so much...the Porfirio Diaz Bed! It belonged to Porfirio Diaz...Porfirio Diaz himself slept on it! So you think "oh, well the bed of a President must be better and bigger than normal people's beds, you know?" It must be embedded with gold, dripping with diamonds and shit. But then you finally see the bed and well, it's just a bed. It's a nice bed. It's big and with a nice design. But it remains just an old bed.

EL NOGALAR
Tanya Saracho

Dramatic
Lopez, 30s

Memo Lopez was once a humble worker in the estate's pecan orchard, but is now a successful entrepreneur, mainly due to his ability to stay under the radar and play all sides of a quarrel. Lopez recalls the meaning of the orchard through a story about Maité Galvan, the mistress of the Nogalar, a formative figure in his life, and one who has shaped his view and place within the Mexican class system.

LOPEZ

My life is written out in the bark of those pecans. That orchard is the first thing I can remember. Me running around with no shoes, carrying those baskets of pecans back to the silos. When I was like, I don't know how old, old enough to feel like I was a full-grown man, my father gave me one of those beatings that break off a bit of your soul. The old man was taking out a whole day of frustrations on my back. Going at it hard as he could with that whip when out of nowhere Maite appears and pushes him off me. She gives him one hard slap on his leather face. She curses something at him and then drags me with her to the silos. She says "don't cry little man." I'm standing there in front of her, bleeding, shaking. And slowly, very slowly she takes off my shirt. Then she starts to hose me down. "Don't cry, little man," she says even when I had stop crying. (Pause) Shit, after that, I followed her like a puppy. Too old to be doing that and I know her parents had said something to her. Well, because she was just divorced and with a kid and well, it wasn't proper. But she didn't care and I didn't care.

We went everywhere together. We... (Beat) One day, I guess it was when her father found her the new husband. That day she took me from cracking pecans, and... she just took me by the river to this little wall the bank makes. She'd been crying. She said, "take off your clothes, little man." Oh, man, I took off my pants so fast. Almost fell in the water. She starts laughing and takes off her dress. I have never... I have never seen something more beautiful in my whole life. With that light that day. With the sun on her. And all of her just standing there. And me tangled on the ground with my fucking pants. She says, "stay there, little man. You can look at me, but you can't touch." So I freeze there. Looking. For I don't know how long. Then she pulls up her dress and runs. She ran so fast, so fast that she left her sandals there. When I went up to the house to give them to her the next morning they said she was gone. That she'd gone off to live in Monterrey where she was going to be married. Just like that, they took her away from me. (Pause) Me and these trees, we're the only ones who remember. Right by that river there. Not far from the bank. "You can look, but you can't touch."

THE END OF THE WORLD
Andrew Biss

Comic
Hank, 30s-50s

The End of the World *is set predominantly in a bed
and breakfast establishment located somewhere in the
afterlife. While there, the play's protagonist, Valen-
tine, meets a number of singularly unorthodox visitors
and fellow guests. Here, he is confronted by Hank, a
swaggering, bigger-than-life Texan who's trying to
convince him to invest in an unusual business venture
he's working on.*

HANK

Okay, I'm just gonna spell it out for ya. I think it's pretty clear
that in this day and age most everyone wants to talk and no one
wants to listen – specially if you're the type to bore the pants
off a herd o' chickens. It's a basic, fundamental human need to
be heard that we all share but no one gives a shit about. Am I
right? And that's a demographic – a discontented demographic
– and a market share ripe for the pluckin'. Right? So here's the
answer: We take people like you – nice enough in themselves,
but kinda bland on the whole…and they know it – these are
smart, self-aware people, mind you – and we offer them, at an
affordable price, the opportunity of having one of our medical-
ly certified surgeons – fully indemnified, mind you – implant
a small plasma TV screen into their foreheads that can receive
real-time feeds from some of the most popular cable television
networks available, right there into that useless empty space
above their eyebrows. (*Beat.*) Imagine it: You're just itchin'
to impart all the tedious details of everything that's hangin'
heavy on your mind to one of your co-workers at happy hour
in the local bar. They're bracin' themselves for an hour or two

of clenched teeth and thinkin' to themselves "Won't he ever shut the hell up," when suddenly, to their great surprise and delight, you produce a convenient palm-sized remote control that gives them the freedom to choose between all the latest news from CNN, up-to-the-minute action from ESPN, or a thought provoking costume drama from your very own BBC, all at the touch of a button. Meanwhile, you – all too aware of just how disinterested your petty life concerns are to your captive audience – can feel free to yak yourself into a frenzy as you bask in the fully committed and rapt attention of your recipient's gaze. It' a win-win situation!

ENTERPRISE
Brian Parks

Comic
Weaver, any age

*Weaver is talking to a fellow businessperson as they
look out the window of their office.*

WEAVER

Look at this! This view from our office so high in the sky. *We*
did this. *Business* built this view. That's what business *does*.
Builds towers that reach into the atmosphere, towers with glass
entrances and soaring lobbies of polished marble, the fruit of
our greatest quarries! Elevator banks – elevator after elevator,
buttons ready to be pressed, each glowing with mystery. Who
knows what button 15 leads to, button 20, 50, or 85! Who was
the man whose brain first fired a Neolithic synapse and thought
of adding a *second floor* to his crude hut? Who took his eyes
off the horizon and looked *up*. A second floor, then a third, a
fourth – till we get architects kissing the heavens with pointy
needles, then epic rectangles of glass. These architects were
geniuses, men with more talent in their silver mustaches than
the rest of us put together. Visions came to them, edifices so
tall they can be seen for miles, by grocers and mailmen, far-
mers looking up from their plows and wishing they could work
in them, away from their manure and poorly dressed wives.
And atop these skyscrapers they attach radio towers. Radio
waves throbbing to every horizon. But traveling upward, too
– into space! Through the ring of planets and great cold ether,
the dark void, speeding through the heavens and white-and-
orange galaxies, searching for anyone to receive their signal.
Anyone! Till finally – finally! – they hit a planet unimagined
by our best astronomers. A planet inhabited by creatures whose

bodies contain not a single element from our periodic table, whose house pets resemble great balls of cottage cheese. But a race besotted with the power of radio! Their landscapes cluttered with antennae, their homes ablaze with dials and knobs, gathered together every night with their offspring, glued to broadcasts from across their globe. And that's how they're sitting the night their broadcast starts to crackle and hiss, then turn to a kind of static, then into *something they've never heard before*. They hear *us*! The consonants and vowels of their language cannot describe it. But they know – they *know* they have heard a sound from *across space*, from a vastly distant planet. They know now they are *not alone!* They hush those balls of cottage cheese and listen to the signals and begin to quiver and shake, then melt a little as they do when excited. They stand and jump in celebration, hugging and melting on each other. Then they go quiet and separate. They stand still and lift their odd optic nerves toward the sky, to their heavens. They reach out and clasp their...claspers, giving thanks for the sound coming from their radio. A sound that started atop a skyscraper – a country song about a pickup truck loaded with beer and hope!

EVERYTHING IS WONDERFUL
Chelsea Marcantel

Dramatic
Jacob, late 40s-early 50s

*Jacob, an Amish man, speaks to his daughter, Miriam,
who is thinking of leaving the community. She has
been sexually assaulted by her boyfriend, and the
rest of the community has forgiven him, but there is
no mechanism within the Amish world for her to find
the closure she needs. The strain of this is hardening
Miri's heart.*

NOTE: "te" = "the." ""Tat" = "that."

JACOB

Forgiveness is te spine of life. If you cannot practice reconciliation, you put us all at risk. In Germany, and in Switzerland, they persecuted us and martyred us. And now, here, they mock us, close our schools, try to draft us for their wars, *(pause)* kill and kidnap our children. And we forgive. Always, we forgive. We do this te same way we do everything. *Gelassenheit.* "Submission." Submission is a bad word to the English. Their lives are built around grabbin' and holdin' on. Our lives are not our own. We surrender everything, from te moment we are born. *(Beat)* I suffered what you suffered, just not in te same way. But I must surrender my right to revenge. I must surrender my right to anger and resentment and self-pity. Bad things happen. They happen quite a lot. And surrender is not te only way to move on. But it is te way we know best. I wish I could show you an easier path, but I have not found one. You must, you MUST let go of te thing inside you tat makes you want to crush him. It's a curse. I am tryin' to take this hardness off your heart, girl. *(pause)* Forgiveness and reconciliation are two different things, Miri. Forgiveness is a choice. It happens in an instant. Reconciliation is a journey. It may take you the rest of your life. But forgiveness must come first. Speak, forgive, forget.

For information on this author, click on the WRITERS tab at www.smithandkraus.com

EVERYTHING IS WONDERFUL
Chelsea Marcantel

Dramatic
Eric, late 30s-early 40s

*While driving impaired, Eric hit and killed two young
Amish men in a buggy. Instead of pressing charges,
the family has taken him in to work on their farm and
live in their barn. Eric speaks to Miriam, 25, the el-
dest daughter of the family, who was excommunicated
from the Amish five years before.*

ERIC

I drink. A lot. Alone. I mean, I'm quitting. I quit. I haven't
had a drink since … I was on about day four of a bender and I
was just not disappearing the way I usually could. There was
still so much of me around. I got into my car. Just to drive
… just to try to outrun… the thing. I was driving for a long
time. Not speeding. Not being reckless. Hours. I had a full tank
when I started. I wasn't really drunk then, at that point, but
I hadn't slept in days. It was about 6:30. The sun was going
down. I was running out of gas. I thought to myself, 'Well,
you'll just run out of gas, and maybe you'll just pull over
on the side of the road and stay there. What would you be
going back to if you turned around?' I was close to here. I
didn't know the place, but the sun was so nice. Nice colors. It's
really hypnotic to drive, around here. The hills and the fields
and… I didn't feel happy right then, but I felt nothing. Finally.
Which is what I wanted. My head was getting light. Lifting off
like a balloon. I felt myself fall asleep, and it felt so nice, and
I really didn't care if I never woke up again. I drifted… then
my whole body exploded. I opened my eyes in a turned-over
car. And I thought, 'you did it. You're dead.' I didn't know

that anyone else was involved until I woke up in the hospital the next day. *(pause)* They were just trying to get home before dark. I wasn't legally drunk when I ran up on the buggy. Just tired. Legally, it was an accident, even though it was completely my fault. Your parents won't press charges. That's why I came here, actually. I asked them to. And they forgave me instead.

For information on this author, click on the WRITERS tab at www.smithandkraus.com

EVERYTHING IS WONDERFUL
Chelsea Marcantel

Dramatic
Eric, late 30s-early 40s

While driving impaired, Eric hit and killed two young Amish men in a buggy. Instead of pressing charges, the family has taken him in to work on their farm and live in their barn. Eric speaks to Jacob, the family's father, about what he has discovered about himself during his short time on the farm.

ERIC

I like the repetitive, physical stuff. I like sleeping in the barn. I like living in my body, instead of my head. I like going to sleep exhausted. And, AND, it's been two weeks since I got here and I don't even think about drinking anymore. You should be charging me for this. Really. I've been to lots of expensive rehab places that weren't half this effective. I really don't want a drink, not at all. I do good work, and I can put my hands on it. I can be in the same room as myself now, and not need a distraction. It's like I've been staring down a long tunnel, at just one thing, but suddenly the tunnel is gone, and I'm looking around me for the first time in years. Before now, my whole life was just want, get, use, repeat -- day after day after day. I can see the bigger picture now. This life is a real blessing. Maybe the first one I've ever had. Things are simple here. It's better. Rules mean something, because people actually care about them.
(he begins to get really worked up, talking quickly)
And the whole issue of what it means to be a man! Ha! Don't even get me started. I look at myself, and I'm just so *weak*. But

I look at you and Abram and the others, and I think of your sons — MEN. I'm going to do that. I'm going to be like that. The work will make me into a man. I might lose all my hair one day, I mean, I probably will lose all my hair, that's hereditary, but I'll have SHOULDERS. I won't be a coward. Not anymore. I won't be so afraid to fail that I don't even try. Not anymore. Not now that I know how to do it right, when everyone out there, everyone I used to know, is doing it wrong. *(pause)* I've been to the top of Macchu Pichu. I've been to temples in Thailand. I went to Catholic school for ten years. And I feel closer to God sleeping in your barn than I ever have, anywhere else.

For information on this author, click on the WRITERS tab at www.smithandkraus.com

FAREWELL TO THE THEATRE
Richard Nelson

Dramatic
Harley Granville Barker, 39

*Harley Granville Barker, all around man of the British
theatre, is contemplating leaving it all behind. He is
in Williamstown, Massachusetts visiting friends and,
possibly, looking for a teaching job. Here, he tells
a professor at Williams College his ideas about the
theatre.*

HARLEY

No tricks. Nothing – "clever." I'm not being clear. For
example, the Oberon. When he says he is invisible. I didn't
have him hide or run off or even turn his back. The other actors just didn't see him anymore. Simple. Do you see what
I mean? And I think *that* should be taught to students. Be
simple. And all that that says about stage design today. How
since really the late 17th century, the theatre has struck up
a rather doubtful alliance with scenic art and artists with a
capital A. And all the harm that has caused. We don't need re-
volving stages, and switchboards, and overly fancy lighting. It
can be so much simpler than all of that. Someone should teach
them that, that's all. If someone isn't telling them in school,
if all they learn about is what they see in the theatre today,
most of which is rubbish. But we all know that. When plays
are kept going now for months merely as "the favour" of the
shirting hotel population. This is not what the theatre can be.
Must be. Once, at a public dinner, and old playwright – I won't
say which one, he's congratulated for the wonderful parts he's
given actors. He stands up and shouts: "Parts! I do not create
parts! I create men and women!" That's what I mean. That's
what I'd teach, what they need to know. If they are really in-

terested in the theatre. Do you think your students would be interested in learning that?

For information on this author, click on the WRITERS tab at www.smithandkraus.com

FATHERS AND SONS
Michael Bradford

Dramatic,
Marcus, late twenties, African-American

Marcus is talking to his wife, Yvette. It is almost a
week after the disappearance of their son, Stephen,
while he was in Central Park with Marcus. Yvette
cannot help but blame Marcus and in this moment is
about to leave to stay with family.

MARCUS

Together. That's how we survive this. Together is what keeps
us sane in the midst of frogs and blood falling out of the sky,
and just 'cause that ain't possible don't mean it won't happen,
but we built a life on this rock between us, didn't we? That's
what you say to the one you lay down with when you give up
that thing that makes you ... you put it in their hands and say
what I got for you is beyond love baby. I got crazy *trust* that
you with guard this like the fifth battalion and you give me
yours and I will keep it like the Alamo and no man made or
natural disaster or otherwise can take this gift you gave me,
nothing but a decree from God and we ain't even nowhere
close to being in a position the hear *anything* from God, personally ... we just here for each other ... and we might even go
toe to toe with God if it gets funky enough but that's how it is
when you love. Yvette please. Hate me, if you can't do nothing
else, hate me. But stay. Please.

For information on this author, click on the WRITERS tab at
www.smithandkraus.com

FATHERS AND SONS
Michael Bradford

Dramatic
Leon, late forties-fifties, African-American

*Marcus and Leon, son and father respectively, are dis-
cussing their relationships with the women in the lives
and Marcus is challenging Leon's version of his story.
Leon decides to instead speak to the core problem of
their relationship and why he is here now.*

LEON

Every story got a little more to it than what you get in the
telling and it don't matter who's telling it. That's how I know
it was me you was talking about. *(Beat)* That's right, I read
your book. Surprised ain't you? Your Aunt told me about it
and I got myself to one of those big book stores and found it.
Whatn't hard. They had set it up in its own little space and I
said I'll be damn! Look at my boy. I was so damn proud. And
they wouldn't even let me pay for it. I had the money. But I
told 'em you was my boy, pulled out your picture from when
you was in the service.
(He takes the picture from his wallet.)
The manager came over and gave me a copy. Just like that.
Couldn't even wait till I got to the house to read it, I was trying
to look at it the car. Drove all up in the damn curb. You know
the last book I read? Hell I can't even remember what it was.
(Beat) I know that was me you was writing about. First word
fell out of the man's mouth, I knew it. And I knew I had to do
something, between me and you, 'cause everything you said
about me, I said about my daddy. Everything I hated about that
man, I seen it me, seem like for the first time, with that book in

my hand. I said right then, my son ain't burying me feeling like I felt about my daddy. But I couldn't put the stuff down and it damn sho' whatn't putting me down. I swear I stayed straight that whole time you was in Iraq, read John 3:16 every morning for you son. And the day I heard you might be coming home I thought, a little taste, to celebrate, might be alright and … When your Aunt told me about your boy, that he was missing, I knew it was time, do something worth something, help you in any way I could.

For information on this author, click on the WRITERS tab at www.smithandkraus.com

FIREPOWER
Kermit Frazier

Dramatic
Neil, 27, African-American

In a Washington, D.C. motel room hoping to soon meet his boyfriend T.C.'s father yet fearful that T.C. is still reluctant to follow through, Neil tells T.C. about the first time he visited D.C.

NEIL

We were on the Mall near the Washington Monument. Us and about a million other folks. And it was pretty hot for spring. We'd been there most of the day. And man were we ever tired and hungry. Starting to get all up in each other's faces and shit. And then somebody begged the teachers to take us to a real mall so that we could at least be cool. Our teachers powwowed while we just hung out. I was sorta in the back by myself as usual. Never was one those class clowns, you know. Despite what you might think. . . . Anyway, I'm just standing there waiting when suddenly I catch the eye of this guy. He's staring at me. A white guy. In his thirties maybe. Dressed like a tourist. And when he sees that I'm seeing, he smiles at me. And I'm thinking, shit, man, is this for real? But just then this white woman, kinda dumpy, comes up to him holding a little girl's hand. And just like that it's gone: the smile, the look, the . . . whatever. All melted into the crowd. It was kinda like it didn't happen. He didn't happen. Like I'd dreamed him up. And when I came back to myself and turned around, my class wasn't there anymore. And you know what I did? I panicked, man. Which was kind of stupid 'cause, shit, I was 17 years old, for God's sake, not seven. But I still felt . . . abandoned.

That my classmates and teachers had deliberately ditched me. I turned around and around like a damn spinning top, started to get dizzy, to hyperventilate. And then pow, I saw them. That is, I saw Carrie's flaming-assed red hair. But when I caught up to them it was like nobody had even missed me. Like it didn't really matter whether I was there or not.

For information on this author, click on the WRITERS tab at www.smithandkraus.com

FIREPOWER
Kermit Frazier

Dramatic
Eddie, 41, African-American

*Having shown up unannounced on his old girlfriend
Joanne's doorstep after a nearly 20-year absence, Eddie tries to explain himself to her.*

EDDIE

Yeah, I've changed. Changed a hell of a lot. And like I said,
and it's the God's honest truth, I really, really missed you. The
whole time. After that first summer back home, when we did
all those things, made all those plans, I went back out to California and got too wrapped up, swallowed up. It wasn't like
I didn't think about you a lot. It was more like I was working
so hard to keep my ass from drownin'. And it was like Eddie
this and Eddie that. Eddie, Eddie, Eddie. Then Melinda got
pregnant and I thought getting married was the right thing to
do. Get married, have the kid, be a man. And then tryin' to go
pro with a family in tow. Rocket for an arm just like my dad,
and they want me to play some scat back defense like all I was
was legs and moves. And then my damn knee went out. Twice.
And suddenly I'm expendable. Gotta get me a regular-assed
job. And I looked around and saw how white my world had
become. Found myself spending more and more time with the
brothers in South Central. Cracked my marriage wide open.
But I couldn't come back home. I was too ashamed. Tail
between my legs like some ole beaten down performing monkey. Besides, you were hitched and gone yourself by then. So
I just gradually booked on out of the country to Canada, then
Morocco, then across Gibraltar to Spain. Odds and ends in

Spain. Hell, you'd be surprised how easy it is to slip into this image of yourself as some sorta sapped-out expatriate. Some beat-down writer or some jazz musician who'd hocked his horn. Or better yet some black power burnout. Especially with my Eldridge Cleaver goatee. And now . . . back home.

For information on this author, click on the WRITERS tab at
www.smithandkraus.com

FIREPOWER
Kermit Frazier

Dramatic
George, 64, African-American

*Having come home late and in a drunken state even
though he's just begun radiation treatment for
prostate cancer, George, former football star and
now Washington, D.C. city council person, speaks
to his young fiancée, Liz—as well as to his two adult
sons, Eddie and T.C.*

GEORGE

I've been sitting down in that bar all evening, Liz. . . . Anacostia. Shoot, I came up there. Lotta folks did. Had me a rocket
for an arm, too. Do you know what it's like to have a rocket
for an arm and then all of a sudden not be allowed to use it?
All that firepower and nowhere to aim it. Can you imagine
how much it hurts? Your arm getting hot and heavy like it was
some kind of sealed up cannon just aching to explode. You
know, when I was younger—not that much younger, mind you
'cause I ain't that old. But when I was younger I'd sometimes
dream my right arm was so humongous I couldn't even lift it.
It'd get bigger and bigger and bigger until it'd sorta push the
rest of me right on outta the bed. Plop. It's a wonder it didn't
just role on off the bed and crush me to death. A man's gotta be
able to use what he has, boys. Use whatever firepower he has.
Your mother knew that, rest her sweet soul. Alma understood
where I was coming from. Always understood. But it seems
like y'all don't seem to know it all of a sudden. f you ever
did. Just look at you. The two of you. But where's my daughter, my little girl? Where's Kathy? How come she ain't here?

Bet you understand that. Know about that. (Pause) Armstrong High School. Yeah, baby, I was the "Strong Arm of Armstrong." I was <u>it</u> at Armstrong, just like my brother had it going on in his head at Dunbar. As for <u>Anacostia</u> High right nearby? Well, you see, white folks claimed it was much to "high" for us coloreds back in the day. Private homes, though. We had us some private homes. Middle class. Ole Frederick Douglass looking over us up on Cedar Hill. And when integration came along we showed'em, didn't we, Alma? Showed'em how we could spread out, make it out. And now they wanna be squeezing the rest of us outta that good ole housing stock close in town. Capitol Hill striving like hell to be a mountain. "Chocolate City melting in the noonday sun of gentrification." And that damn Councilman Pierce having the nerve to condemn me for compromising, for so-called "trading gay rights for housing rights." Hell, I've got a right to trade on it. We been traded on and traded on and traded on for far too long. So he better not be gettin' all up in my face like that. I do what's right for black folks. To hell with his queer ass. He and all his AIDS-spreadin' constituents. Talkin' about how I promised to stand with him. Well, I stand with black folks first! Black folks and morality! Always have, always will.

For information on this author, click on the WRITERS tab at www.smithandkraus.com

FIREPOWER
Kermit Frazier

Dramatic
Eddie, 41, African-American

In frustration and anger, Eddie has just thrown his completed autobiographical manuscript onto a coffee table in front of his accusatory father, George.

EDDIE

You wanna know why? You wanna know who, what, when, where, and how? It was in my head for so long. Stuffed all up in there. Pounding, taking up space, sucking up oxygen, keeping me awake all night and then sending me crashing down. Like some sorta . . . hallucinogen. Like when I'd do mescaline back in the day. Tripping for hours that seemed like seconds and then sleeping for more hours that stretched on like days. The glaring sun, then the stars and the moon. Over and over and over again like a cycle that never seemed to wanna take me along with it. And I'd pace up and down and up and down whatever confine, whatever little room, whatever space I'd secured, commandeered, carved out of someone else's place—some woman's, or even some admiring guy's. Me. The expatriate, the black power figure manqué. Shit, the powerless figure just black and lost in a string of cities, towns, villages, a badgering bunch of foreign languages taunting me, teasing me. Languages which I never studied, didn't have to study, 'cause in school I was so cool, a star athlete just like you, Dad. Until suddenly, one night in some dim light in, in, shit, I don't know. Switzerland, I think, the pressure had built up so much I was either gonna die right there or let it out, open up some hidden door and just let it all pour. And I took up this pen and grabbed this pad I'd been using to calculate my expenses, my allotment for the day, my figuring out how much I was gonna have to beg, borrow, or steal to get through to the next night, and I wrote . . . I fuckin' wrote in big bold capital letters: "I SEE DC."

For information on this author, click on the WRITERS tab at www.smithandkraus.com

FOMO
Rhea MacCallum

Comic
Jack, late 30's and up.

Jack panics when he realizes that his wife, Ellie, is mentally spiraling into a deep funk after spending too much time exploring social media websites.

JACK

Oh, no. No-no no-no. This can't be happening. Not now. You're not due for your next existential crisis for another three weeks. I'm not prepared. If you're going to melt down on me I need to go to the grocery store. There's no ice cream in the house. No cupcakes. Is your favorite bathrobe clean? Do I need to run a load of laundry? Oh, God, laundry. I can do this. What do you need? Are the Kardashians available on demand? What about *The Housewives*? Or *Million Dollar Listing*? We can Netflix *Love Actually*/ Would you like to sit through your millionth viewing of *Love Actually*? You love it when Hugh Grant starts dancing. I can set you up with your favorite movie butter popcorn and the foot massager so you can catch some Nativity Lobster and Billy Bob Thornton as President while I run to the store. What was it that pulled you out of the last funk? Was it the Chunky Monkey or the Cherry Garcia? Or both? I'll buy both. Just in case. Why be frugal when it could spell disaster. Should I light a candle before I go? Where's your relaxation candle? Family room? Bathroom? Never mind, I'll find it. Or something like it.

FOMO
Rhea MacCallum

Comic
Jack, late thirties and up

Jack tries to convince his wife, Ellie, to make life decisions for herself based on her own true desires versus the social media activity of others.

JACK

Friends? I don't know most of the people you're talking about. Can you really call them your friends? They're acquaintances, maybe. Former friends, okay. Former colleagues, former classmates. People who were part of your life at some point but aren't anymore. Not really. You don't spend any time with them, live and in person. This social media thing, it's not natural. It keeps you connected to people who would have otherwise faded away from your life. And it's not like you really know what's going on in their lives. You're only getting the highlight reel of accomplishments and vacations, the things they want you to know about but it's an incomplete picture. There's so much more to living than what people post online. Don't you remember what the world was like before social media? When if you wanted to catch up with a friend you called and heard their voice or grabbed a drink after work together? That was friendship. You made time for each other. Made plans with each other. Hung out and ate and listened to one another and connected, really connected. If it wasn't for social media do you really think you'd even know what was going on with half of those people? You'd maybe see them every five years at a reunion and that would be enough. Our parents, our grandparents, they never tried to stay connected to everyone they ever met. It's too much. Life is too busy to even try to keep up with every random person from your past.

If you haven't talked to someone since elementary school why are you letting social media drag them into your present day life? So... so what if someone's a grandma again or goes on vacation or out to eat or whatever? That's great for them, but you shouldn't let it affect you like this. If you want to do something, then let's talk about it. Let's do it, but let's do what we want to because we want to and not because someone you knew once did it and posted it online. Okay?

FRIENDLY'S FIRE
John Patrick Bray

Dramatic
Todd, late 20s

*Todd is dressed as an astronaut ready for SciFi night
with his best buddy, Guy Friendly. Guy, a "bee-herder"
suffering from PTSD after a tour of duty in the first
Gulf War, is suffering from hallucinations tonight,
desperately trying not to relive the last moments of his
brother's life. His imagination, something he never
bothered with, is starting to run wild. Todd attempts
to talk Guy through his darkest hour.*

TODD

The way I see it, life is entirely imagination. You know? It's
why I never cared about getting rich. Never meant anything.
Imagination gets us through the rough patches. You know? TV,
movies…games in the yard? All that kid stuff. That was great.
My favorite thing was to play gangsters. Al Capone. I had a
toy Tommy Gun and everything. There was a girl who was a
tomboy that lived across the street. Wore overalls. She always
wanted to be Frank Nitti. She did a neat impression of the guy
on the old Robert Stack TV show. We grew apart a bit in high
school – that's just life. She started listening to loud music she
could dance to. I went in for radio control stuff: cars, helicop-
ters…other things. Still have a bunch of them, too. So, anyway,
one night I'm out walking the dog, and I see her in the window. Her bedroom window. She's getting undressed, and I'm
looking at her. She's about to take off this black bra. I didn't
know what to do. I mean, her lights are on, I can see her. There
was a streetlight, so I stand right under it, and I…I clear my
throat. Loud. I do it again. She unhooks the bra from the back,

and I give a real loud cough. She turns and looks at me. I look at her. I give her a little wave. The moment kind of suspends. I don't know what to do. She takes the bra…the rest of the way off, and I see her. I see her. She turns off the light, and disappears into darkness. I still have the light over me. You know what happens next? That damn dog, "Sugar" mama named him, a little Beagle Chihuahua Jack Russell mix; he lifts his leg and pisses on my boot. I look down, and say "shit." And I hear laughing from the dark. I shout back "thanks, Nitti!" And walk away. You know, I think that's the reason I never got married. I met the perfect girl way too young in life.

For information on this author, click on the WRITERS tab at www.smithandkraus.com

GUNPOWDER JOE
Anthony Clarvoe

Dramatic
Benjamin Franklin Bache, 30s

Fears of foreign terror are running high and the president is enraged by his critics in the press. Congress has passed a set of repressive laws, the Sedition Acts, in an effort to stifle dissent. Benjamin Franklin Bache (male, 30s), an outspoken newspaper editor, has been arrested. As he is questioned by, and is simultaneously trying to get some answers from, a federal official, he explodes at the absurdity of his situation.

BACHE

So, writing anything in opposition to the Sedition Act is a violation of the Sedition Act? If I write that the Sedition Act is unconstitutional, your judge will find that I have violated the Sedition Act. If I write that the Sedition Act is unwise policy, I am questioning the wisdom of our leaders and I have violated the Sedition Act. When I tried to publish the Congressional debates about the Sedition Act, I was arrested for printing statements criticizing the Sedition Act. I was quoting Congressmen who are our leaders! If I write that the Sedition Act forbids me to write that someone has criticized the Sedition Act, I have violated the Sedition Act. That's quite an act, that Sedition Act. Good God, sir! Is it a crime to doubt the capacity of a President? Have we advanced so far on the road to despotism in this country that we dare not say our President is mistaken?

For information on this author, click on the WRITERS tab at
www.smithandkraus.com

HAPPY BIRTHDAY ADAM SCHWARTZ
Cary Gitter

Comic
Adam, 30

*It's his 30th birthday and Adam, a struggling actor,
has just been "broken up with" by his best friend, Liz,
and his boyfriend, Jerry, for being such a narcissist.
He suddenly stands up on a chair at the restaurant
they're in and addresses the room.*

ADAM

Ladies and gentlemen! Fellow diners! Good evening. I apologize for interrupting your meals. My name is Adam Jacob
Schwartz. I am an actor. Today is my thirtieth birthday, and my
best friend, Liz, and my boyfriend, Jerry, have just broken up
with me. They say I've been self-obsessed, insensitive. Fine.
MAYBE THEY'RE RIGHT. But I wanna say this, to them
and to all of you: perhaps the world NEEDS people like me.
Perhaps you need neurotic, witty, attention-starved Jews to
stress you out, to make you laugh, to remind you you're alive.
What would we do if we had only responsible, professional
adults? Or sweet, handsome dolts? Our culture as we know it
would perish. So for the excitement and humor I try to bring
you, I say: you're welcome. And for your failure to honor it, I
forgive you.
  (He makes a grand gesture of absolution.)
As for me: I'm going to keep auditioning! I'm going to get my
big break! And one day I will share the Golden Light of My Personality and Talent with All the World. MY NAME IS ADAM
SCHWARTZ. HAPPY FUCKING BIRTHDAY TO ME.

For information on this author, click on the WRITERS tab at
www.smithandkraus.com

HOW ALFO LEARNED TO LOVE
Vincent Amelio

Comic
Tony, 40

Tony Vallone tells Alfo Idello, his childhood friend, that marriage is not as complicated as it seems. Alfo desperately needs advice to get married in order to inherit the family bakery.

TONY

Marriage is like . . . eatin' pizza. You're sitting at home with nothing to eat - you start thinking about pizza cause your stomach's empty but your head's full. So you order a pie cause you weren't getting any – and when you're not getting any you dream to fill your head. So you give the delivery guy a ten dollar tip cause this pizza's gonna change your life! You eat three slices. Now your head is empty and your stomach is full. You got five slices left over that won't leave your house. You can't throw 'em away cause you're not a killer. You can't give 'em away. And selling 'em makes you a pizza pimp. But then you realize . . . you like having the pizza around . . . it's *your* pizza. So you start to take care of it. You wrap each slice in aluminum foil. You put each slice in the back of the fridge to keep it fresh. You check on 'em before you go to bed. Then in the morning, you got cold pizza for breakfast. And it's good – it's not the best pizza of your life – it's not toe-tingling, mind-blowing, make-me-scream pizza. It's good decent pizza. But it's there for you. It was there at night to put you to bed and it's there in the morning to wake you up. It's your pizza - - and you can deal with that. That's marriage!

For information on this author, click on the WRITERS tab at www.smithandkraus.com

HUNGARIAN COMEDY
Susan Cinoman

Dramatic
Baysha, 30-40, a Gypsy

Baysha has broken into the home of Angala, a farm woman, alone in her house. He has been watching Angala for a while now, and has designs on both her and her house, which, through mysterious means, he knows belong to him. In this monologue, Baysha explains to Angala how he has become a lost soul in need of something that he contrives for her to give him. He tells her the story of his friend, who had been left in his care, and died. The speech is part lamentation, part seduction.

BAYSHA

Have you ever been so close to someone that you didn't know where you stopped and the other began? That's how it was for me and my friend. He was like a brother... a little brother to me. Like a child, an innocent child. I had known him since I myself was a boy. We were messy un-scrubbed children together, just the type that you wouldn't want in your house. It's not the point, really... what I mean is when you have something like this in your life, this closeness, this responsibility and then it's gone... it changes something about you. It leaves a hole. And maybe you just wander around aimlessly trying to fill that hole or trying to just forget that hole. But it's there—that hole. It's just always there. And even if you're happy or drinking or rich or wounded there's this small feeling that your friend, your reason for doing things, is gone. Sometimes you're even nervous that you've forgotten your friend because you're feeling free or making love to a beautiful farm girl but then something reminds you that yes... he's gone. And you wish and believe that he's somewhere else, that he's being taken care of, but you're not sure. You're just not really sure. You don't want me to feel pain because you've come to like me and I've come to like you. And you know me only just a little. Think of how much I would do to protect my friend who I like so much and knew for so long. Think of how I'd try to right any wrong that was done to my friend when he was alive. He expected me to protect him and I didn't. He's gone. And I'm here with you. And there are things that I'm supposed to be doing and I'm not. Maybe I'm not very good at anything. It doesn't matter anymore. Maybe no wrong was really done. Maybe he just got sick and died. Just like that. I came here to avenge him. I came here to kill a farmer! To rape a farmer's wife! But I was cold. And hungry. And I've decided that I like you. And I want you. You see?

For information on this author, click on the WRITERS tab at www.smithandkraus.com

HUNGARIAN COMEDY
Susan Cinoman

Dramatic
Baysha, 30-40, a gypsy

*After spending the night with Angala, Baysha confesses
to her his original plan for her. He then informs her of
how his plan has changed and reveals his true nature.
He assures Angala that he could never have done her
any harm and, much to his own surprise, his true wish
is to marry her and be with her forever.*

BAYSHA

Look, I wanted revenge when I came here. I wanted to
ravage the farmer's wife and make the farmer feel small, like
they make us feel. In my mind, I wanted to kill a farmer! But,
I ouldn't do it. How could I ever do that? I'm not a killer. I
planned things carefully in my own spontaneous way. I was at
the bar, out of funds, feeling angry, very angry. I'd seen you
in the market in the town. Smelling things likes cheeses and
squeezing things like lemons. You were all wound up like a
top. I wandered back to *this* house, *my* house. I thought I could
almost hear the cries of my poor, slow, innocent friend. As he
died. When I couldn't get him to a decent hospital... He cried
out. "Avenge me!" That's what I thought he said. So I knocked
on your door, acting just like you thought a murderous, lunatic,
frightening gypsy would be! I wanted to scare you! And then
I just wanted you! You understand? But I was wrong about
what my poor friend called out to me. He didn't say, "Avenge
me"... he said, "Angala. Angala." The thing I never planned
to happen, did. I fell in love with you. You see? Love is mysterious! We started out as foreign to each other as the stars to
the earth! But not anymore. We can be ourselves finally. I'm
actually quite tame. Life will be good. Yes, there will be bills.

And laundry. I can be a pig! Like any man! I like to watch football, I'm not that unusual! We'll make a permanent situation of this. You, my wife. I've never been very legal up to now, but sometimes a man has to face the facts. He mates for life. And he signs a piece of paper to do it. And what's more, the paper costs him a fee collected by the state. What a turn of events!

For information on this author, click on the WRITERS tab at www.smithandkraus.com

IZZY
Susan Eve Haar

Seriocomic
Ned, 38

Ned, son of the tyrannical Izzy, addresses his father who is allegedly on his death bed. Liberated to say what he has always felt, Ned lets loose. But Izzy isn't going down that easy. Ned and his sister Denise struggle to get something, anything from their father. They are going to get Izzy's blessing even if they have to give it to themselves.

NED

It's my thirty eighth birthday, Dad.
    (imitating IZZY's voice)
"Happy birthday to you, Ned!"
Thanks, Dad. Or maybe you'd say, "Happy birthday to you, son," that's a little more affectionate. Wow, I feel so good.
    (He laughs.)
Well, this is it. The beginning of a new life. Yeah. It's kind of scary, Dad, and yet it's kind of great. Now I can do things-- travel, if I want to. Wow. Maybe go to Hawaii. You used to say there were women there with nipples like chocolate moons in Hawaii. NO MORE CHOCOLATE MOONS FOR YOU DAD! Cause it's my turn now and I'm not going to fuck it up. Wow. You don't look so good, Dad. I guess it shows in the end -- what you do. And Dad, you've been greedy. Oh yes. And it's not nice to be greedy. It leaves you bloated and old, and wrinkled like an elephant scrotum. And dead. But you're not quite dead, are you, Dad? Not yet. YOU MADE ME WAIT, YOU OLD BASTARD! Well, I have been waiting thirty eight years

for my life. I have been reading comic books and smoking weed and just waiting for my life to begin. IT'S MY TURN NOW!

          (shouting in IZZY's ear)
ARE YOU SLEEPING, DAD? HAVING SWEET DREAMS? You were not a good dad, Dad. Not that I don't admire you. You were a great man, a man who employed thousands of workers. Even if most of them were Chinese political prisoners. And Dad, you had it all. You earned it, or cheated, or stole it. BUT, YOU SUCKED THE LIFE OUT OF ME, YOU FUCKING VAMPIRE! DIE!

KISS
Guillermo Calderón

Dramatic
Youssif, 20s-30s

*In this over-the-top monologue, Youssif is expressing
his love for Hadeel in order to make fun of the melo-
dramatic style the play is criticizing.*

YOUSSIF

I just I want to be part of you, Hadeel. And I know that you
love Ahmed... but let me tell you... It is totally human to love
two men at the same time. Try to love the two of us. You know
what I'm talking about. You can love two men at the same
time. You can. The heart is a big muscle and yours is bigger
than normal. I know. And it happens to a lot of women. They
are in love with one man and then one day they meet another
man and they don't know why but they hate him. Why? Because they secretly like him. And that is the beginning of a
second love. They feel it's treason. But they can't stop. They
can't. They love two different men. And then naturally there
will be broken hearts, screams, tears, even blood, the same old
story. But, Hadeel... listen.... even if you love him you have
every right to choose the man who really makes you happy.
Not the one who promises you a wonderful future but the one
who shows you happiness here and now. And that man is me.
You know that. I've seen it in your eyes. Right now you can
despise me. You can even hate me. But that's just the beginning of something... You have two loves right now. I know
it. Choose me, Hadeel... Choose me. Forgive me for being so
honest. I just want you to be my wife.

For information on this author, click on the WRITERS tab at
www.smithandkraus.com

L'APPEL DU VIDE
Molly Kirschner

Dramatic
Quentin, 18

Quentin, a college freshman, is speaking to his new roommate, Simon. He has spent the last several minutes trying to convince Simon that the whole room belongs to him, Quentin, as he needs a medical single, and insisting on putting up a poster of Nietzsche, much to Simon's horror. After assuring Simon that Simon's personality is "flaccid and women aren't attracted to that," Quentin continues to assert his dominance over Simon, describing his own great successes with women.

QUENTIN

We're roommates. We gotta help each other out. I'm just trying to show you as much of the ropes as I know. Which isn't a whole lot, I'll admit. But once I liked a girl. Yeah. In high school. Elissa. She was on the model UN team. I think she was also a model. If she wasn't she shoulda been. Anyway I used to pick white and purple violets for her. I'd tape them to her locker. Sometimes dandelions. I think she liked it because after a while she caught on and started smiling at me in the hallways. But then winter came and there weren't any more flowers but I did find this dead baby snapping turtle so I taped *that* to her locker. And she acted all weird about it. Like she stopped smiling and even looking at me in the hallway even though she obviously saw me. And one day I saw her and before she could breeze by me I said, "Hey, Elissa! What's your problem?" She didn't say anything so I explained to her that the flowers were *also* dead they were just better smelling. I didn't kill that baby snapping turtle, but I *did* kill those flowers. Flowers don't die when they dry they die as soon as you pick them. After that she didn't act any different but I could tell she realized I was right. She went to the prom with a jock who was a jerk. Anyway, I'd never go out with a girl who didn't get Nietzsche. I met him first. And the thing you vegans don't get or have an impossible time digesting is that plants are conscious and you have to kill to live.

THE LAYOVER
Leslye Headland

Dramatic
Dex, late 30s – early 40s

Dex's flight has been cancelled due to inclement weather and he can't get out of O'Hare Airport until tomorrow morning. The airline has put him up in a hotel for the night. Here, he confesses to the woman who was sitting next to him on the plane that he had a revelation about her before they got on the plane.

DEX
I lied to you. I saw you. Before we got on the plane. I saw you at the gate. Waiting to board. Everyone around you was so busy. Keeping themselves busy. And you... you were staring at nothing in particular. No book. No phone. You looked--Misunderstood. Like a profoundly misunderstood person. And, I know this doesn't make any sense, but as I was standing there, looking at you, I skipped to the part of the story where we already knew each other. And I was the person who knew you best in the world. I could identify every flicker in your pupils, every slight change in your mood. Detect it as you felt it. Anticipate every rise and fall of your chest. I was suddenly that person for you. There have been many times when I could've stopped this. Conversation. Many times I could've exited gracefully. And no matter how, I guess, "right" it would've been to walk away... there was... a nagging feeling I had... Why can't I be that person right now. Please look at me real quick.
(she does)
Oh man. So... do you believe... that without knowing me... I could be that person? Just for tonight. I don't want to spend years growing close then drifting apart. I want to be the one who knows you. Right now.

THE LAYOVER
Leslye Headland

Dramatic
Dex, late 30s-early 40s

Dex is trying to find a woman was sitting next to him on a plane, with whom he had a one-night stand during a weather-induced layover. She then disappeared. He has tried to find her, but has learned that everything she told him about herself was a lie. He is speaking to a private detective he has hired to locate her. Since Dex is engaged to be married, the detective has asked him why he wants to find her, what his endgame is.

DEX

I can remember everything she said that night. And those things repeat. In my head. Over and over. Like the lyrics to a song. So even though she's not a part of my life... she. Is. Now. You know? On a very real unconscious level. It's like compartment syndrome. It's when... if you injure yourself, you know, hurt or twist or sprain your arm, or your leg, and, at first, you don't think there's anything wrong cuz there's no external damage. So you don't go to the doctor. 'Cuz you don't think you need to. But with compartment syndrome, blood has stopped going to the muscles and nerves in the injured limb. And then this pain begins. It's so, uh, slight. It sets in like a dull hum and builds steadily and stealthily into this deep constant pain. But with no external damage to point to... the pain... seems like it's only in... your... head. But if you don't treat it, you have to amputate the limb. (pause) So I guess, yeah. I'm trying to treat it. That's my endgame. The symptoms I'm experiencing... Not love but pain. It's exquisite. And so out of proportion to the initial injury... it leads me to believe that something significant... is happening to me.

LE DERNIER REPAS
David Eliet

Dramatic
Louis, mid 30s-mid 40s

He is speaking to Robert. They are both French chefs.

LOUIS

There was this girl sitting all by herself at a table on the other side of the room, twenty-three, twenty-four, maybe a bit younger, a bit older. Very pretty in a plain unadorned way, dark sad eyes. One of the German refugees clinging to the shore, staring across the ocean towards inaccessible freedom, with the enemy crowding in on their backs – our backs. There was a small orchestra, locals I suppose. Not very good by any standard, keeping together and in time was about the best they could manage. I got up, walked across the room and asked the girl if she wanted to dance. I'd never done anything like that before, just gone up to a total stranger and asked them if they wanted to dance. No, I was always too shy, too afraid of rejection, I guess. "Mademoiselle, would you care to dance?" At first, she rejected my offer, merely shaking her head "no." She probably thought I was some aging lothario. Unasked, I assured her I was a married man with a daughter of my own, not much younger than herself, and that I had no ulterior motives, that I simply wanted to dance, just one dance and then I would be leaving. She hesitated, staring down at her plate, like she was trying to move the food around by sheer mental concentration – pot au feu, as I recall. Finally, maybe because she was afraid I'd never go away, she agreed to "one dance." At first, we were both a bit shy and awkward, and to speak truthfully, she was not a good dancer. But after a few minutes we were managing to move across the floor with a bit of grace. I held her loosely so as not to frighten her. she told me she was living not far from there with her grandfather, that her parents were in Holland. She said she was a painter, that she was painting her life story, and was staying at the hotel trying to finish up the task she had set herself, while there was still time. She was twenty-three, twenty-four, and she was painting her life story, as if her life had already reached its climax. And I wondered, even if she managed to finish it, who would there ever be to read it, to gaze upon those pictures and piece her story together? And even if they did, what would they understand? How could anyone ever understand what it was like to be twenty-three or twenty-four, and to know your life was over, and not because of any sickness of the body, but simply because you had been designated as "other," without the least bit of interest in who you are, what you are, what talents you might possess, what qualities as a human being, what dreams or aspirations live in your soul, what memories in your mind, what loved ones hold you dear. No, it's not comprehensible. How can anyone understand that? Near the end of the dance, she rested her head on my shoulder and finally surrendered to the music, to my leading. For a brief moment, very brief, we moved as one, this young girl and I, this sad young girl standing on the edge of the abyss looking down at the end of her life. And I could feel her, I could feel her entire being melting into mine with everything else fading away. It was one of the most perfect moments I have ever experienced in my life.

LES FRÉRES
Sandra A. Daley-Sharif

Dramatic
Fedji, 30, Haitian-American

Inspired by Loraine Hansberry's Les Blancs, Les
Fréres *tells the story of three estranged brothers of
Haitian descent, who come home to Harlem for their
father's final days. Troubled memories filled with anger and abuse come rushing back as they deal with
their father's death. They are forced to deal with how
each choose to deal with memories, how each have
escaped, feelings of abandonment, betrayal and loss.
This speech is delivered by the oldest brother Fedji,
as he and his brothers catch up after years apart, he
tells them about his work as a Jehovah Witness Elder,
working in the community.*

FEDJI

I teach African Studies. Not so surprising. Nothing different,
really. It's all teaching. Just that, when I'm an Elder, I teach
a congregation. My *own* congregation. I'm in and about the
community, investigating matters *in* the community, a lot of
our own people, but it's black, white, Indian, Asian, you name
it. And... I decide disciplinary actions. You see, my brother
is blessed. He's in Harvard. But I teach brothers, just like
you. Men - *not* so blessed. Incarcerated in Bayview, Lincoln,
Rikers... They don't have better. They don't know better.
Some from Haiti, Puerto Rico, Dominican Republic... I teach
them the healing words of Yahweh. I share the word with these
young and *old* men. Men who occupy dark jails, live in self-
imposed prisons, live in stark hospitals and facilities... Some
are drug abused. Hiding their pain. Some sitting on street corners. Some right out there, on St. Nich.

(as he gestures to the outside).
Just last month, a young brother, Malcolm, he's been in jail more years than out... He's 18 years old! A child, really. Still, a child of God. Not much younger than Christophe. Serving life for *first-degree murder*. His family came to me, they said, Elder Ewens, "He's a thug! A disgrace! A menace to our community." You know what? I recently, I baptized him as one of Jehovah's Witnesses. Now, he knows the love of Yahweh and recognizes the scourge of his pasts. Praise Jehovah! I am a witness to the courage of these men. I didn't see much of that before I became an Elder. Courage. Of Men. The life-changing power of the Bible is outstanding. My desk - my walls, are papered. They are full of certificates and awards, for the work we do. For men like Malcolm.

LOOK AT ME (RUFF, RUFF)
C.S. Hanson

Seriocomic
Omar, 21

Omar, a journalism student in college, talks to his former middle-school teacher whom he wants to interview for a news story.

OMAR

I have never forgotten you. I used to dream about you at night. . . . At night. During the day. All the time. Mrs. Shepherd, you changed my life. I used to fall asleep at night thinking of your classroom, dreaming that all the books were mine. I could hear the sound of your voice speaking perfect English and I pretended that you were near me. I don't want to interview anyone else. You're the woman who opened up my world. The Mrs. Shepherd that I've never forgotten. You were different from the others. There was no one like you. You were -- you are -- a woman who wears nice clothes. Especially now. This is how you dress in your home! . . . You must never change. I'll never forget how, whenever I whispered in class, you would stand beside me – And when you did, you smelled like springtime -- a scent that I later learned was Chanel No. 5. I was a middle school boy whose mother was still in Mexico City and I used to pretend that you were my mother. I'd see billboards advertising Chanel and they always made me think of you.

LOS SAMARITANOS
Sandra A. Daley-Sharif

Dramatic
Denver, early 30s, Mexican-American

*Denver is speaking to his pregnant wife Rosa.
While he tries to convince her to pack up and move
to California, he finds out that not only has his gas
station been robbed, but 10 illegals were found hidden in the shed behind the station. Does Rosa know
anything about this!? What else might she be hiding?*

DENVER

We all agreed. They pass through *once* a month. Lately, it's
been getting more frequent. More frequent means more dan-
gerous for you and me. We can't risk that. Now look at what's
happened! And 10 of them Rosa! What the hell!? We have an
agreement. If we don't stick to the agreement, nobody's safe.
I've got to go down to the fucking precinct. Rosa, what am I
going to say? Don't you think they're going to figure out I was
hiding ten illegals in that shed? What am I going to say, Rosa?
And you and Monte pick a night that we get robbed. On the
same night! Why did Bloom take them to the precinct? Let's
hope he just pack their asses up and send them back across the
border. 'Cause God help them if he accuses them of stealing
that money. Ten grand. I got there this morning, found Manny
on the sofa tied up, had peed in his pants, and the back office
turned upside down. They broke into the safe box and took
all the money from the week. I straightaway called the police.
Called Old Man Beaver. We waited till the police got there.
They didn't even *go* near the shed. Tavo's right, Sgt. Bloom's a
damn Sherlock Holmes and Pink Panther rolled into one. He's
a fucking ninja! ... Now this. I don't know. With all that's been

going on in town lately, it could be anybody. Folks are pissed off. They're scared. Looting. Looting their own neighbors. Getting desperate. And losing jobs. I don't know. It's probably some gang. I got to go back to the station.

LOS SAMARITANOS
Sandra A. Daley-Sharif

Dramatic
Sgt. Bloom, 50s, Arizona Police Officer

Sgt. Bloom is speaking to Denver. He long suspects that Denver, his wife Rosa, and the famed Monteverde are Los Samaritanos - sympathizers aiding, transporting and hiding illegals.

SGT. BLOOM

I am onto you. I hear them in the cell whispering, *Monteverde*. *Monteverde* floats above the murmurs. Some kind of Mexican messiah, they say. I hear them… and his samaritan friends. Then, I hear *Denver*… whisper, whisper, whisper… Did I hear correctly? The white Mexicano. I hear *Denver*. I hope you are smarter than that Denver. And now you are running off to California. These illegals you shuffle across, they come here with their hands out. Beggars! *All* of them! In droves. Like cattle. They take good paying jobs. Pay no taxes, to boot. Instead they run here, ready to steal what we Americans have already broken our backs for. They *scratch* along the highway, dying in the desert. I pity, the fools - the traitors, who call themselves Los Samaritanos, who *give* them water, supplies, and safe haven. Dead most of them. These illegals. Fools. Days in! Bodies piled high in the unforgiving desert. Take this as a warning. I have got my eyes on you, on the gas station, on Gustavo, on Constanza. I've got my eyes on both of you.
(He walks to the door. Turns.)
How rude of me, thanks for the delicious water, Rosa. *Muy delicioso!*

LOS SAMARITANOS
Sandra A. Daley-Sharif

Dramatic
Denver, early 30s, Mexican-American

Denver is speaking to his wife Rosa. She has accused him of stealing $10,000 from the gas station. He admits to it, and here's why...

DENVER

A couple of weeks ago my father drove into the gas station. Like he didn't know I worked there. *Whatthefuck!?* Or like he did..., but there was no *surprise* on his face. Nothing. And there was *Denver* right on my chest!!! It was surreal. *Pero, nada.* I looked at him, and I hadn't really seen him since, since I don't know, since I was a kid. *Pero sabía que era mi padre.* I would recognize him anywhere. I was looking into those same eyes. *Mis ojos.* I'd been dreaming of the day I would stand in front of him *cara a cara. Y allí estaba*, sitting in a pretty *fucking* Cadillac convertible with a V-8. And, he said a whole lot. And, check this, he had this girl sitting there next to him. Younger than you! Heading off to Vegas to *marry* her. And I'm thinking, *Whatthefuckdoyouwant!?* I said, congratulations! Shit! He gave her a diamond ring. I saw it, sitting on her finger, glistening in the sun. She was over ripe and pretty. She was pregnant. Like you. Pregnant for his *old* ass. Heading off to Vegas! It was all I could do not to kill him. Put my hands on him! NICE WHITE SHIRT!! Head butt him! Fucking knock him senseless. Leave him for dead!... in front of his *soon-to-be-bride.* Rosa, get this - He offered me a job – actually, *she* offered me a job. SUZANNA! *That'shername!* My 23-year-old step mom. He told me my luck's going to change... or it could, and it was time to do something different. *Youbetter-*

fuckingbelieveit! So…, I took a pause…, and I thought about you. I thought about my son. I thought about California. Gustavo. Finding… my mother's family in Mexico. I figured, *Hell, I've got nothing to lose.* That night…, I know… I know… I looked hard at that money… sitting in the safe. I figured, *This is enough to give me and Rosa a start for something new.*

LOST AND GUIDED
Irene Kapustina

Dramatic
Sami, 30s, Syrian

SAMI

I will be honest with you. Things are very, very bad, actually. I stay here day and night, I stay here... I will stay here till the end. And listen... Our Arab brothers, our Arab Muslim brothers are abandoning us. The Arab world is turning their back on us. They are supposed to be our neighbors, but they refuse to take us. In the whole gulf region, they say they accepted millions of refugees, they are *lying*. They never accepted them, they didn't accept anyone. And if you went there, Syrians are threatened every day. You never have job security. My cousin just left a job after ten years. He worked in a famous oil company. They just threw him out. Because he's Syrian. And I have to get a visa to all of these countries. They refuse. They say ... the official decision to not allow any people from Syria to go and get a visa. It's a very, very small amount, small number of people who are getting visas. I tried Saudi Arabia, I tried Emirates, I tried to go to Oman. I did more than ten job interviews. I was the first in my class, in my graduation exam all Arab countries? Of some 20 countries! And what? First, they say, "Yes, you're hired, sign the contract, now you will wait for the visa." I have copies of them, of my contracts, I still have them. There is this big hospital in Saudi Arabia...The head of the OBGYN department, till now she is sending me emails...till now she is communicating with me, sending me emails, she tells me, "Sami, I need you to come but I can't control the visa issue." So there are no visas for Syrians! But these are old news, and you know them. What I am saying is... is that I am not going anywhere, brother. I am staying right here, till the end. I am staying here, with my patients and my people.

MULTIPLE FAMILY DWELLING
James Hindman

Dramatic
Stuart, late 30s-40s

*Stuart suspects his fiancé, Tia, has had a more color-
ful past than she lets on. In order to find out the truth,
he confronts Tia's best friend, Kelly. He hopes that by
showing her a more vulnerable part of himself, she
will tell him the truth about Tia.*

STUART

Tia tell you I was married before? Lasted two years. We're
married about a year when we're invited to another wedding.
Thirteen months, to be exact. And for some reason, out of
nowhere, every bridesmaid, every grandmother is fighting to
drag me on the dance floor. They've got me doing shots of
Tequila…leading the conga line. And then it hits me…Where's
Catherine? That was her name. I look in the parking lot,
the kitchen; I peek in on the wedding down the hall. All those
women…the bridesmaids, the grandmothers, are distracting
me because they know where my wife is. I go up to our room.
Figure, maybe she isn't feeling well…and there she is…and
this guy…and they're so drunk they don't even… And I don't
get mad, I don't. All I can think to say is, 'What the hell are you
doing?' And she says, 'What does it look like I'm doing? I'm
fucking the best man!' They'd been hooking up for years. And
I still wasn't mad. Embarrassed, maybe. *(Beat)* 'God throws a
stone before he throws a rock.' That's what my old man tells
me. I should have seen it coming. Should have seen the signs.

For information on this author, click on the WRITERS tab at
www.smithandkraus.com

1980 (OR WHY I'M VOTING FOR JOHN ANDERSON)
Patricia Cotter

Dramatic
Will Moore, late twenties, African-American

Boston, Massachusetts 1980, just months before the election of Ronald Reagan. In the tiny four-person, "John Anderson For President," campaign office Will looks for the missing office key, as he describes to Kathleen, a young volunteer, his morning run in with a racist Boston cop. He was accosted by two police officers after trying to return a wallet to a white woman.

WILL

I had a little incident on the bus today. There was a woman who got off at the same stop as I did. A white woman, which is important for our story today. When she got off the bus I noticed that her purse was open. I actually noticed that on the bus, and I was going to say something, but I just didn't. When we were getting off, her wallet fell out of her purse. Pretty much landed on my foot. I picked it up and I yelled out to her, but she didn't hear me, so I start following her. And all of a sudden she starts running, so I have to pick up the pace. I hear yelling and I thought it was other people, telling her to stop, you know? People who'd seen what happened. I'm just behind her, holding it out, offering it up, about to say: "Here's your wallet, lady. You're welcome." When out of nowhere this big, fat red faced cop is right behind me, and he tackles me - right on the street. The fat fuck. Sorry, but that is actually the most accurate description of this individual. Then I'm on the sidewalk, face down, and this other cop has his gun pulled out and is standing over me. And they're both yelling "Stay on the ground." "Put your hands over your head." Which of course I was already doing, because they have a gun and I'm not an idiot. Then the one cop, I guess the brains of the operation says: "Give me the wallet!" And then I get it. Of course. I toss it to them and I tell them: "I was running toward her. *Toward* her with her wallet." By this time all these people are watching - including the wallet woman. So I look at her and say: "You dropped your wallet." She's just staring at me. Then she gets it. She sees it a different way, not what she thought she saw a scary, black guy chasing her, but she sees it the way it happened. She tells them that, yes, I was running toward her, but she didn't see me running after her with her wallet, she saw me running after her with a gun. Her wallet was pink by the way. So I was chasing her with my big, pink gun. Finally they let me go. Nobody says, sorry. Sorry we completely screwed up. Sorry we left you on the ground for forty minutes, while half of Boston walked by, nothing like that. All he says is: "You're free to go." Like that was enough. Like they did me some big favor. I'm from Evanston. Chicago cops? Please. But it's not like it is here. It's different. This town has a very specific and unapologetic attitude about it. It's kind of schizophrenic. Sorry about the bigots, but try the clam chowder.' You can elect the first black senator since Reconstruction and in the same state, another black man gets stabbed by a white guy using the American flag.

NO ONE LOVES US HERE
Ross Howard

Seriocomic
Washington, 19, Native-American

*Washington has been staying with the Beaumonts
these last couple of weeks. He has just killed Mrs.
Beaumont's father during the wake for Mr. Beaumont's
mistress, who he has also killed. With all now revealed
and being pressured to leave, Washington explains
himself to Mr. and Mrs. Beaumont.*

WASHINGTON

You both may look at me in your lives right now with, I don't
know, some suspicion . . .and Mr. Beaumont, with no doubt,
some regret, but by no means . . . to my coming here, could
anyone describe your marriage as healthy. I'm doing all this
for you, Mrs. Beaumont. In you, I saw a beautiful flower surrounded by nothing but disease. As a keen pruner yourself, I'm
sure you know what I'm talking about. Mrs. Beaumont, you're
the most beautiful woman I've ever seen. Ever since you first
came into the video store, I've been obsessed with you. You
would come in regularly, and for the twenty-four hours or so
after those times you came in, I was unable to either sleep or
eat. I took more shifts, came in to help when I didn't have
a shift, and sometimes I would just go there to hang out because I didn't ever want to miss you. I always had access to
your address but it was only when you started to come into
the store less and less that I decided to come here. It was just
making me crazy. My mind was racing. "Have they switched
to an online service?", "Are they just happier with their cable
movie package?", "Do they now only watch on Blu-ray? Or
have they just made a conscious effort to read more?" All these
questions I asked myself, and it was killing me. Fortunately,

you did have some movies out that were due back and so I came over here. When you both invited me to live here, I could not believe my luck. This house, you, it's really all I've ever wanted. I love you, Mrs. Beaumont. You may not be quite right in the head and maybe neither am I. Maybe Mr. Beaumont isn't either. But at least you and I have a soul.

For information on this author, click on the WRITERS tab at www.smithandkraus.com

OH, MY GOODNESS
Cayenne Douglass

Dramatic
Tom, 60s

TOM

Um… okay, well, basically there are a lot of protein wastes that we produce as a society and don't use. A considerable portion of those are left to aerobically compost and that produces a lot of nitrous oxide and methane emissions. These are toxic greenhouse gasses that hurt the environment. But they don't have to, not with technology! So, what I, what my lab was working on when I left was utilizing biology and biological principals to solve engineering problems. Anything that comes from a nonrenewable source we tried to find a renewable way to make it. We looked at municipal waste and agricultural waste, like manure, sewage, plant matter, and then we had a variety of different bacteria and microorganisms that we would manipulate. For example, we could engineer the metabolism of bacteria to eat the greenhouse gasses, and in doing so, get them to excrete alcohol compounds, and those compounds can be used as the building blocks for an alternative fuel source! See, waste is just potential energy. Energy that can be used for fuel, or life, or to fuel life. Isn't that neat? It's pretty spectacular to think of things like that. It's so satisfying to know, to feel, when the wind blows, I'm getting electricity. When the sun shines I'm getting energy and hot water. When it rains I'm filling up my tanks to water my garden. It's right there. It's right in front of us. I mean, if you step outside, if you look, really look; you'd see that it's worth protecting. You can't help but see this incredible abundance, this sacred divinity, this fantastical beauty, this, this God-like… It's not about religion, it can be, but for me, it's just about… It's what makes me feel connected. I see that divinity in nature and that I'm part of it, not separate from it. Sometimes I'm just, I'm overwhelmed by, there's this abundant benevolent force that washes over me, through me, and I know, in my bones, in my body, that there's something greater we all stem from. It's the thing that's gotten me through, that lets me trust and believe everything will be okay. That there's a natural order to things… even through the chaos… even through the darkness…

For information on this author, click on the WRITERS tab at www.smithandkraus.com

ORIGEN
Anderson Cook

Dramatic
m00t, late 20s

m00t is a programmer in his late 20's with osteoporo-
sis imperfecta, or brittle bone disease, which has left
him stuck indoors with limited mobility as the slightest
bump on the street would be enough to fracture his
bones. His rage at his parents for mistreating him, his
disease, and the world for rejecting his difference, has
manifested into misogynistic anger towards the women
of the world who won't pay attention to him. Here, m00t
speaks to a younger friend whom he is teaching to de-
sign a website, and explaining to him the supposed pe-
rils of manhood and feminism along the way.

M00T
Did you see that Anita Sarkeesian got like a $300 million dollar partnership with Intel? Fucking absurd. The Feminist Frequency girl, the one who has made a career bitching and moaning about the representation of women in video games when she doesn't even play video games. Her whole fucking campaign is just about trying to make other people as miserable and unhappy as she is. I mean, God forbid she actually learn a useful skill and build her own video games. Of course not, 'cause she majored in women's studies and now all she's equipped to do is complain about stuff. Dude, that's the tip of the iceberg. It's not really about the video games. It's about the fact that although we're already rejected by society, by all the chads and dudebros who think we're pussies and losers, by the women who would rather be dead than give us a chance on a date, and now we don't even get loser nerd culture. She has to come in and sanitize it for her tastes when it isn't for her, was never for

her, and after she fucks things up for a while and nobody buys these shitty video games with strong women, like, I dunno, getting abortions and taking down the patriarchy, she's gonna be gone. And all the shit that made our lives barely tolerable will have been ruined.

ORIGEN
Anderson Cook

Dramatic
m00t, late 20s

m00t is a programmer in his late 20's with osteoporosis imperfecta, or brittle bone disease, which has left him stuck indoors with limited mobility as the slightest bump on the street would be enough to fracture his bones. His rage at his parents for mistreating him, his disease, and the world for rejecting his difference, has manifested into misogynistic anger towards the women of the world who won't pay attention to him. Here, m00t and his friend Jason have just doxxed (leaked the personal information of) a women who was arguing with Jason on the internet, and Jason begins to feel guilty. m00t reassures Jason that they were justified in what they did.

M00T

Do you think she's going to get fired because some anonymous person accused of her selling drugs? If her boss is that stupid, we did her a favor. I just posted it to a couple of chans and other people did the rest. I mean, this stuff if publicly available. She should be more careful. A lot worse things could have happened than this. All people did was say things on the internet. I've been thinking about this a lot lately. I think that people who don't code, who don't really understand how computers work, they think that we have literally put real life onto computers. They think it's exactly the same, somehow, so the rules should be exactly the same. When it's not, at all. And if you actually knew how programming works, how machine code and assembly language and HTML and CSS and your jquery and ruby and php shit all comes together to show your pretty little Twitter window, you'd realize how fake it is. It's not like talking to someone at all. You don't have to stand there and be scared of them. There are no consequences. There can't possibly be. You can't punch someone in the face if they make fun of you, and that's what they hate. They hate that people who are losers and who have been made fun of forever in society for how they present themselves are finally able to push back.

A PATCH OF BLUE
Lisa Kenner Grissom

Dramatic
Joe, 30s, African-American

Joe, a postman, is in a church, speaking to the assistant pastor.

JOE

I broke my TV the other day. Smashed it with a baseball bat on my front porch. Then I set that piece of shit on the sidewalk for everyone to see. To see that I don't want to live in fear. Why? So people will leave me alone. So the bruthas won't come around and stir me up. Barely got three channels and they all spouted bullshit. White guy on channel four? He looks *positively stoked* reporting black men getting killed every day / white police getting off. *"Now back to you, Jessica, and the weather--sunny all week!"* Sunny for who? We're holed up in our houses--straight up depressed. So I smashed my TV and it felt good. Now I know what you're thinking but I can tell you--I am not a violent man. I'm just your average guy with a government job trying to provide y'know but sometimes the situation calls for it. And lately the situation is calling for it *a lot.* So you can try to convince me I'm praying...that God works in mysterious ways. Well it ain't gonna work with me. But if I can look at something that takes me away / something that gives me an ounce of peace / and it happens to be here, what's wrong with that? I apologize. For the language. The trash. I'll just deliver the mail from now on.

THE RECKLESS SEASON
Lauren Ferebee

Dramatic
Simon, 22

Simon is speaking to his younger brother Terry, 19. Simon has just returned home from a four-year stint in the army where he served two tours in Iraq. He's discovered his mother is dead and Terry is obsessed with a video game about ancient warfare. Just prior to this scene he has overheard the town drug dealer, Flynn, warning Terry about how many of the Iraq veterans come back mentally disturbed.

SIMON

Let's say you just saw your best friend get blown up by an IED planted in a pile of trash on the side of the road. And someone gives you a tip that there's a kid at the end of the road that gets paid money to set them out. And so you find out where this kid lives, and so you raid their house at midnight and everyone is screaming and crying and you've got that kid and you've got his dad and you've got his mom and you've got everybody up against a fucking wall and you look in this kid's eyes and he's shitting himself he's so scared. What's the big picture vision there? What's the plan? What's the strategy? You're *motherfucking* right that's not what the game is about because if that was the game, no one would play it. No one in their right mind would play a game like that. The game is a fairytale. The game is fiction. And you just eat it up, hour after hour, how noble that shit is, because it's got a fucking story and it all makes sense, it all fits in a little fucking box. But you wanna play a war game man? Play Russian roulette with a twelve-year-old and let me know how you sleep after that.

THE RECKLESS SEASON
Lauren Ferebee

Dramatic
Flynn, 22

Flynn is speaking to Lisa, 23. She and her husband are both army veterans who served in Afghanistan, and her husband has gotten addicted to meth, which Flynn sells to him. One night, high on meth, Flynn comes to the truck stop where Lisa works to absolve himself of the guilt he feels.

FLYNN

It is all a part of this pattern, I mean, your husband left you because you didn't love you anymore, and Terry's mom died because nobody loved her, and she wanted to die because of that, Lisa, the thing that connects them is that they were not loved enough, that you did not love your husband when he was hurting. You couldn't save him from those fire-breathers whose eyes bled sand, and you couldn't save him from his nightmares – but I did, Lisa, I helped him, and I helped their mom, and it's me, I *help*, *I* fill them up with what feels like love, or even better than love, actually. I did that. It's like a *superpower* I have, like, I can give them the chemical compound for the love that *you can't give them, so...* but I feel bad now, Lisa. I feel bad because now I look at you, and now you have that, there is a cavity inside you, the absence of love, and I am here, I am here, I am here to help you, to give you the thing that you need. Do you know how he loves you, Lisa? I mean, he knows what pure love is, why can't you just figure out how to love someone? I'll tell you why, your heart is deficient, it's too human, you know? You don't love enough.

THE RECKLESS SEASON
Lauren Ferebee

Dramatic
Flynn, 22

*Flynn is speaking to the audience. He has just been
rebuffed by Lisa and is now coming down off meth.
As he does so he is breaking apart the world of the
play and re-forming it, echoing how meth changes the
chemical responses of the brain.*

FLYNN

Are these the hands of someone who's a bad guy? No. No.
No. These, what I see, extending from my hands, are these
like, points of light that they like, they connect me with all of
these people and I just have to pull a little or they pull a little
and I'm there and they're there, and we together - it's like, you
know, in those superhero movies, like the bat signal, like, that's
what my hands are but like the bat signal in this case is like totally, like the end of things. The end of things, end of love, and
that's where I come in. I rearrange the world, not just in big
pieces but I mean like, in molecules I rearrange the world, and
it's my world and I change it, I change the world, I change
the people in the world, until the most ordinary sounds are
symphonies and a fucking shithole is really a mountain and
on the mountain is enlightenment so close you can punch
it right in the fucking face, you can give enlightenment a
bloody nose. And you should, too, because enlightenment just
fucks you and leaves you right? And the symphony spins an
spins and spins – no that's not- no, don't – there's like, you
can bend it all, you think you're stuck, and you're stuck, and
you're stuck, and you're stuck you know, there's just, there's
something holding you back and then you have to get above

it. I heard you give visions, like end of the world shit, and I don't want that – don't, just let me hold onto this. I just want to hold on to this, I just have to remember –

(Something invisible socks him in the chest and he falls down.)

Oh. Oh shit. How did I never see before that the sky, it's made of this fragile glass, like the kind you can almost see through, the kind that shatters and can never be repaired because it's in too many pieces, and you have to be so careful with it, even holding it up you could break it, and it has within it the end of itself, like, at any moment, just this could all end. (Beat.) I think I'm disappearing.

THE PERFECT SAMENESS OF OUR DAYS
Michael Tooher

Dramatic
Soldier, 19-26

In the grip of PTSD, the Soldier has taken a Gardener prisoner in the mistaken belief that he is an enemy from a forgotten battle. After being repeatedly asked by the Gardener why he wants to hurt him, this is the Soldier's reply.

SOLDIER

You want an answer? Here's your fucking answer. We've lost lots of people, Ali. Men and women. Good people. People with futures. People who joined up because they just wanted to do their time and get a little money so they could get an education or start businesses. Or just chase their dreams. People like me. And a lot of them are no longer here. They are dead, Ali. Dead. And those of us who are still here are really angry about that. Really angry. We're angry about what your raghead brothers have done to us. We're sick of saying goodnight to our buddies and discovering them dead in the morning, slit open ear to ear. Put yourself in our place, Ali. Thousands of miles from home with an enemy that can appear and disappear at will. Once, you've seen the shit come down, it makes you hard, man. Shit that would have made you blow chunks before you got here becomes standard operating procedure. People can become used to anything. I know I have. And when you've had a friend, a buddy, someone you care about, someone who was very much alive a second ago, suddenly stone dead at your feet, well, you'll do anything to anybody to make sure that doesn't happen again. Anything.

THE PERFECT SAMENESS OF OUR DAYS
Michael Tooher

Dramatic
Gardener, 45-50, Middle Eastern

Desperate to distract the deeply troubled Soldier from his plan to commit suicide, the Gardener offers to tell him about his garden if the Soldier will share the wartime incident that left him so damaged. When the Soldier finally agrees, the Gardener speaks lovingly of his garden.

GARDENER

For thousands of years this fruit has been our sustenance, our income, our salvation. My father taught me these skills. This orchard connects me to my ancestors, to my history and to my people. My orchard started with seedlings, planted carefully. Yet from the beginning of their lives they create illusions, because the tree starts to fruit very rapidly. But it takes almost five years of careful care for good fruit, fruit suitable for the marketplace, to develop. Much like having a cat, one must have a good relationship with your trees. Not enough attention, they will fail to produce in abundance. But part of me senses that the trees do not care to be attended to too much. To me it seems as if it offends their dignity. In the summer the early harvest comes. My trees will fruit up to three times in the harvest season. When the trees flower they do so modestly, as a woman does when she first shows you her affection. Soon my orchard is filled with white and red, as the trees celebrate life. The colors are a promise from the tree to give more. And it does, my friend, it does. It is not only a food, as a medicine the oil of the apricot has been used for centuries to help treat the sick. And the fruit, and I can tell you this as we are both men, always reminds me of the delicate, most secret part of a woman. Imagine the joy of this place at the harvest. To be surrounded by these shy females in their full ripeness. Is that not paradise for a man? But what I love the most is the ritual of my orchard. At each point in the season I know what has been done, what needs to be done and what will come. Sometimes in the orchard I feel as if I am thousands of years old, with all the experience and knowledge that come of that great age. There is a peace to this place. A comfort of knowing. The peace, the perfect sameness of the day and the days without end.

RAW BACON FROM POLAND
Christina Masciotti

Seriocomic
Dennis, 20s

Dennis has just been sentenced to a 90 day inpatient treatment center after a violent outburst with a co-worker. When his Iraq combat-veteran mentor comes to visit, Dennis lets him know how it's been going.

DENNIS

I thought I walked into "Someone Flew Over the Cuckoo's Nest." They have us drawing pictures in pyramids, our life ten years ago, knowing how far life is, you're here today and gone today. I can't take three months sitting in these rap sessions. They have us sitting around on these ratchet couches. Like a cult of Hohova witnesses or something. When people stand up to talk, the couches are so old, they fart. That's exactly what it sounds like. The air conditioner shoots out ice. You hear a crack and ice goes flying across the room. No one says shit. They're all kissing the sorry ass of that Counselor Ken. He has no idea what he's doing. Mr. Egotistic. Someone asked where he lived and he said, "I don't feel comfortable sharing that." He thinks we need to follow him home to kill him? I'll slit his throat right outside this building. Anger management is a coloring book. They gave me a box of pencils and a book called: Coloring the Mandela. Do you know mandelas? It's a circle. You fill up the circle with the little things. Some artists are good. Those things are sold in galleries. But they use it to help the brain of a person with a nervous thing. Focusing on tiny details. They say, "Start coloring." They give me a coloring book to cure me, and they think *I'm* sick.

For information on this author, click on the WRITERS tab at
www.smithandkraus.com

ROAD KILL

Karen JP Howes

Seriocomic
Sonny, mid to late-30s

Sonny is a bounty hunter who had dreams of being a stand-up comic in Las Vegas but things didn't work out. He was never very funny, so his day job as a security guard at a manufacturing plant turned into a night job as a bounty hunter. His latest assignment is to track down and capture a Native American activist. The two stop off at a roadside diner in the middle of nowhere.

SONNY

Do you know who hired me? Important people. Government people. You know what they told me about you? They told me you drink diet Dr. Pepper, which means you're a hypocrite because there is nothing about the moon and the earth and nature on the ingredients list for diet Dr. Pepper. Ya know, your file calls you a political activist and says you're starting to make trouble that jeopardizes the peace and well-being of this country. How come it is that people like you say, "I'm a Native American" or "I am African-American." Even stuff like "I'm homosexual" or "I'm a female" -- and they have this pride thing going, and I'm supposed to have this respect thing. But if I say "Hey – I'm a Caucasian male," I'm what? I'll tell you what. I'm the bad guy. I'm the reason for the generation gap and the gender gap and the widening of the social classes. I'm even the reason we got minorities to begin with 'cause I'm what makes up the majority and you can't have a minority with-out a majority. But because it's my fault we have minorities I don't have majority rights. No, I'm the one with the minority rights. Equal opportunity my butt. You think I got *any* opportunities? Well I kind of like moccasins, Beau. However, what keeps me from getting a pair of my own is that a lot of people, me being one of them, think dancing naked with paint on your ass is a hell of a way to make it rain. Nature? What -- Dancing with Wolves? *(laugh)* I'll tell you about nature, though I hate to be the one to break it to you. It sucks. An apple on a billboard and a peach on a water tower. Communing with nature is a hike in some State forest with mile markers. It's an emissions test on your car and a chat group to save the polar bears.

Lawrence Harbison

ROAD KILL
Karen JP Howes

Seriocomic
Jami, 22-25

*Jami is a recent college graduate who is ambitious
and thrilled about stepping out into the world and
working his way up the ladder in journalism -- except
the world isn't hiring. Still ambitious, Jami has carved
out a niche as a small town reporter. He is talking to
a beautiful Cuban immigrant dancer who he wants to
feature in the lifestyle section of his newspaper.*

JAMI

I have degree in journalism from the University of Michigan,
but only 52% of journalism graduates were able to get a full
time job last year. The average salary is $28,000 and you have
to pay your own health benefits. So I thought I'd start with
this county paper as a stepping-stone. But the stones here are
actually microscopic pebbles. Not one murder in the whole
year I've been on the desk. The upside is you should feel safe.
There's a lady in the bathroom, and I think she wants a fried
egg sandwich and a side of bacon. She's very large so you
should use cannoli oil instead of butter when you make the
eggs. Maybe microwave instead of fry. We don't really know
her. She ran over something in the road and it blew out her
tire. How about clams casino? That's not Spanish is it? You
need to eat Ms. Llorente. Roadkill. See that's the kind of news
we get here. It's not a real story. We don't have Indians. We
have irrigation problems. Sometimes, a billboard falls over.
I was banking on serial killers and escaped convicts. America's heartland with all the ailments and psychoses of the whole
country bottled up, exaggerated and packaged into a deceptively perfect small-town in America. You have no idea the

dreams I had. Pulitzer. Prime-time special guest. Keynote speaker. Panels. Documentaries. Before I got on board, my paper covered the entire county with four pages. Eight thousand square miles. Do you understand how lame that is. Then I add a lifestyle section and we upped our page count to 24 and increased circulation to half the 85 population. You might want to take out an ad. Lifestyle is hot. It's like reality TV. People want to read about other people. This is the middle of America. It's a void. A microcosm of everywhere else. A steady dustbowl. Sand sweeping across the plains in gusts to cover the marks made by the cars and the footsteps that came during the day. Does something happen when there's no trace of it? If it occurs and then is gone, was it ever here? I'm not talking about "if a-tree-falls-in-the-forest." That tree lies there. It's there tomorrow for someone to trip over it. It decomposes and feeds the seedlings that grow into other trees that fall over years later. I'm talking about who notices, which is why I'm a reporter, a writer. I keep account and don't let things go unnoticed. You don't understand the newspaper business. We have a narrative. We have drama like one of those Hollywood pieces. This is a Hollywood piece, Ms. Llorente. It's the kind of news that sells papers and is picked up by television. It turns regular people into stars. You swim from Cuba. Hitch hike from Miami. Give life to small town America. Revive an entire county and it's all because of the American dream of success and love and happiness. You work hard. You're pretty. You dance. You do all the right things and right things will happen for you. But -- is the American dream still out there? It started on the coasts. Ellis island and the California Gold Rush. Then it went everywhere. It became the mindset -- Cattle in the Great Plains. Cars in Detroit. Oil in Texas. Technology in San Francisco. But what does it do? It fades from the edges, dissipates throughout the country. Thins out. Becomes nothing more than a dot. And here we are. Poof! Foreclosures, unemployment. Is the dream still there? The American fireman and immigrant dancer. My pebble has become a stone.

Lawrence Harbison

RUNNING IN PLACE
Joshua James

Seriocomic
Trevor, 20s.

Trevor defends the idea that homemade apple pie like Grandma used to make is, in fact, a compliment.

TREVOR

No, no, it's a compliment, I mean, not the age thing but a work thing, nobody does stuff like this anymore, homemade pie, home-made cakes, everything is frozen and microwaveable. Most people don't have the patience to make something like this. That's something about our culture that I've been thinking about. No patience, no responsibility. We want everything now, fast food, fast cars and instant messaging. We want everything done for us and done quickly so we can get on with enjoying our lives. And we want that enjoyment to start NOW. We want the fireworks NOW. We don't want to stand in line, we don't want to be put on hold, we want to see the doctor NOW. That's why there are so many divorces these days, because people want the love and happiness to start NOW. They say, I paid my money, I got the license, I want my happy marriage. When it starts to get shaky, they say whoa! I ordered a happy marriage, not this one! I want my money back! If they had put the kind of time and care into their relationship as you did into making this pie, if they rolled the dough themselves, if they peeled and cored the apples themselves and timed the baking just right, by the time they were ready to take a bite, it would have tasted great. Instead, they said, let's have pie and slapped the ingredients together and wondered why it tasted like shit.

For information on this author, click on the WRITERS tab at
www.smithandkraus.com

SHOOTER
Sam Graber

Dramatic
Jim, 40s

Jim reveals to his range instructor the reason he decided to take an evening firearms course, while contextualizing the internal solitude he feels after social abandonment by his two close friends.

JIM

You asked why I'm here. I didn't live up to whatever men are supposed to be. But I never thought she'd leave. For some guy she met through my friends. Driving the fancy whatever at his fancy lakeside...my daughter decided to walk out as well. That was the real kicker, when Sophie decided to go. And friends aren't supposed to take sides but my two close buddies I grew up with, the ones who it shouldn't matter now about which one has the cars and houses...I guess it's been a long time they've all been walking out on me. But that's nothing new. Life walking out on me. Because the thing is, the real thing is that every day you feel less a man. And what is being a man today, what is that? I know what it used to be. I'd sure like to know what it is. At least she left me the dog. Probably because the new guy's allergic. But what happened was I was home one night keeping myself occupied by whatever twenty-four ounce could fit in my hand when I noticed the dog hadn't come back, and I went outside to yell for the dog, the only living thing in the world that hadn't walked out on me, when I see coyotes. At the edge of the yard. Toeing the curb. Blood on their lips. And they were smiling at me. With blood on their lips, laughing at me, as if to say being a man didn't just walk out on you, it full-on *ran away* from you and it's never coming back. The coyote faces like the people I know, the ones I thought I could always count on to be there. Laughing at me. I'm sorry but when my dog got taken that was the moment when I felt like something right here finally collapsed. Like everything finally got ripped out and was falling out. And I wanted so very badly to grab, in my hands, to fire back, to *squeeze*.

For information on this author, click on the WRITERS tab at www.smithandkraus.com

SHOOTER
Sam Graber

Dramatic
Jim, 40s

Jim hosts a party at his house and the only attendee is Gavin, a young high-schooler enrolled in an evening firearms course with Jim. Jim unknowingly validates Gavin's hidden motive to perpetrate a shooter-massacre at the high school. Ultimately, in the course of the play's chronology, Jim and Gavin exchange fire before Gavin can carry out his intention.

JIM

Lately it's like everything's about making everything more complicated. You get older you'll see that. The older I get the more I can't stand noise. People yelling. It's like someone shouts they don't realize they're raising the alarm. Everything's more complicated. So I've been kind of working on simplifying things. I think it's all simpler once you have a plan. You got a plan? Without a plan things get difficult. Without an idea of who you are and what you're after. I'm always seeing myself driving along, just easy highway driving, when all of a sudden this white van comes out of nowhere and I slam into it and it's horrible. Sorry, it's a dream, I forgot to tell you that. And when I wake up I'm like: I'm the one making the dream. I should know what's coming. Like there's two of me. Fighting for control. My own sweet enemy. So to sort out the two of me I've been working on a plan. You really don't have a plan? Should think about it. When I was at the high school I didn't have a plan. I had tests and confusion. Not what man needs, you know? You should. You think you're a man right now but you're not. You don't realize you have to fight for it. I've had to fight for it. We've all had to fight for it. 'Cause we sure aren't born with it. You're like what is fighting for it, right? You think it'll just happen, it'll just show up, all you have to do is be there. My Dad died and I kind of stumbled along and the whole time I was like what is it? Because what we read about and what we're taught, and then what we see on the streets? I'll tell you. I'll tell you. I'll give the answer but you still won't know, but I'm still going to tell you. Because the truth is...things have changed. They won't tell you but things have changed. I mean some things haven't changed. Earn the money. Provide the house. Bring the food. And *discipline* and/ and/and *consistency*. That's all the same. That's been for ages. That's nothing new. But what's changed is now how *we're the joke*. All those screens and shows telling how *we're* stupid. You know what I'm talking about. You know. We're on the same side. The same team. Threatened. Endangered. See them come in here and tell us *we're* like that. Because *we* still know how to get it. And to get it, it has to be done. So let me ask: how are you getting to the range without a car?

For information on this author, click on the WRITERS tab at
www.smithandkraus.com

SMART LOVE
Brian Letscher

Dramatic
Benji, 24

It's the eve of Benji's parents, Sandy and Ron's, 25th wedding anniversary. Or, what would have been if Ron hadn't died of a sudden heart attack 7 months ago. Benji, a brilliant MIT Phd student, has returned home in the middle of a stormy night, surprising his Mom not only with his disheveled appearance but also with a very human-like Artificial Intelligence version of his father. This speech is right after he has unveiled his life-like father. A speechless Sandy struggles to understand while Benji explains how he made Ron.

BENJI

We all have computer parts. Our brains are basically naturally wired hard drives. Which is why the phones in our pockets are actually more reliable extensions of that biological hard drive. I mean, who bothers to actually remember phone numbers any. And Dad's brain - this Dad, him, right here. The brain is the exact same as Dad's brain from before he died. My team and I input tens of thousands of documents -- four hundred and seventy-one of dad's journals, dating back to when he was eight years old, six hundred and eighty-nine of the audio tapes he was always using to record his random thoughts and ideas, essays and term papers he wrote in high school, any and all video and pictures of him, tons of letters -- lots of business letters, queries about his inventions, patent applications, rejection letters - sorry, Dad, had to include those. All of my journals, my memories of us went in too - and, of course, hundreds of thousands of emails and personal letters. From him to others, others to him. He actually had kept one hundred and fourteen letters you had sent him, did you know that? Love letters. I input those myself - you were really a beautiful writer, Mom, some really beautiful metaphors. And then of course great strides were made in building the body, the skin, the hair - all made from his very own DNA. We had another lab do that. But the real leap -- the one I personally worked on the hardest, was mapping his brain. Filling it in with billions of pieces of hard data, And that, that right there, is where I've made a glorious leap. Most important, when mapping the brain, is being able to map the nuances. Beyond the 'one plus one equals two' stuff, it's the connections we make -- in a nano-second. The flexibility, elasticity, the ability to plan, to problem-solve. To learn from the past. The immense creativity and adaptability that defines a human being.

For information on this author, click on the WRITERS tab at
www.smithandkraus.com

SMART LOVE
Brian Letscher

Dramatic
Benji, 24

*This speech is toward the end of the play. A sobbing
Sandy has just told Benji that Ron has to go back to
MIT, that she will not marry him, that it's all over. Benji,
is holding Sandy's new boyfriend, Victor, hostage with
a gun until she agrees to marry Ron again. Ron is an
android copy Benji has made of his deceased father.*

BENJI

Where do you think all of these things come from, your brand
new toys that Victor bought you? Who do you think INVENTS
them?! Do you think these things just appear -- on a billboard or
a commercial or Best Buy!? "Oh cool, another awesome thing to
improve the quality of my life" - swipe, pin number, it's yours!
The Invention Genie strikes again!! No. People spend years on
it. Very smart people like me and, and like Dad - we work eighty
hours a week to give you what you want! We memorize your
preferences, remind you what kind of music you like - make
the pictures of you, me and Dad at a Tigers game automatically
pop up on your computer too -- yay! - you *love* the Invention
Genie!" And you should. You should bow down and pray to the
gods of MIT and, and, and to me! You should bow down and
thank ME! YOUR SON! FOR BRINGING YOUR HUSBAND
BACK FROM THE DEAD!! That's him, right there - your Ron!
My dad! ...that's my dad. He is right here with us now - alive and
happy and, and...I want him here. I miss him. Mom. Don't you
miss him? Please let him stay, Mom...please let him stay...

For information on this author, click on the WRITERS tab at
www.smithandkraus.com

SPEECHLESS
Greg Kalleres

Dramatic
Addison, 25-30

Addison's father, a renowned and respected journalist, has had a stroke. In his confusion, confesses to Addison's sister, Clair, that he thinks he may – or may not -- have molested her as a child. And while Clair doesn't buy it, Addison can't get it out of his mind. And when he meets Clair's boyfriend, David, for the first time, he unloads...to David's massive discomfort.

ADDISON

It's just, it's a mind fuck, you *know*? Not saying he did anything. But just the fact that he thinks he *could* have. That it's in his head. I mean, that's enough to mess with you. He *sees* himself doing it. Watches it. Over and over. Every night. That he thinks this is who he is. (*Beat*) Because there are even things *I* remember. Little things that I never thought much about but now it's like... Like I remember going into his office once when I was like six? And you weren't supposed to do that, you know, go into his office when he was working; it was like a thing. And he looked at me with this like really strange look. He didn't say anything it was just this...*look.* At the time, I thought it was just that he was pissed that I'd interrupted him. But it always haunted me. I mean, I remember it. To this *day.* And now I think about it. That *look.* And I don't know, you know? And I'm thinking this stuff and I'm *annoyed* that I'm thinking it. But it's like the way it's infected him – it's infected *me.* And, I mean, *you* know who he is. Which is why it's so fucked up because then I'm thinking, like, "what business did he have, really, running all over the world, writing about the plight of struggling brown people!" No offense. I mean, he grew up in Tampa! You know? He was a coddled white kid. His father was a successful lawyer and he worshipped him! So, why? Is it because he felt guilty for something? Or is it because all the violence he researched -- and even *witnessed* at times – infected *him?* And I hate that I'm thinking this but the man just shot himself with an antique Chinese handgun because he couldn't handle the guilt so ...it's hard to not be infected by that.

For information on this author, click on the WRITERS tab at www.smithandkraus.com

STRANGE CASE
Don Nigro

Seriocomic
Mansfield, 30

In London, in 1887, Richard Mansfield, the great American actor, is trying to persuade Robert Louis Stevenson and his wife to allow him to perform a stage adaptation of Stevenson's book, The Strange Case Of Dr. Jekyll and Mr Hyde. Stevenson is not sure he wants to get mixed up in this, or even if it's possible to do it onstage, but Mansfield, a bubbly, energetic, charismatic fellow, has just demonstrated his ability to transform himself into the monster Hyde, before their eyes, without makeup, genuinely terrifying them, and now has bounced back immediately into his cheerful, con man self. He is impatient to get the thing on the stage. Stevenson, still a bit shaken by the transformation into the horrifying Hyde and back, has just asked him how he did that.

MANSFIELD

Acting. That's my job. There's a whole army of people inside everybody, actually. With actors and lunatics, these other persons inside us are just a bit more likely to bob to the surface now and then, as it were, like a corpse in a fish pond. The human soul is like a cornucopia. A smorgasbord. And no makeup. No tricks. Well, some jiggling with lighting, certainly, but essentially, I'll do it with my own physical instrument. I will contort my features. I will extend my lower jaw. I will become nearly a foot shorter. Trust me. I'm working it all out. It will be absolutely bloodcurdling. The audience will audibly gasp. Women will faint. Men will give birth. Elderly bankers will clasp their chests, call for their mothers and drop dead on the spot. I'll be the sensation of twelve continents. The greatest theatrical triumph since Aeschylus wore high heels. All right. That's enough. Time is money and I don't have any. Even as we speak I have personal knowledge of at least seven pirated dramatic versions of this book ready to go on the boards. And those pirating bastards won't pay you one cent of royalties, whereas I will make you a handsome payment for the rights, a very generous percentage of the gross of the net, minus expenses, after taxes, every full moon there's a Thursday. We'll work it all out. But we've got to get the jump on them. In the theatre, timing is everything. Well, that and pretty women. And timing is also everything with women. But that is a tale to be told another time. We spend our years as a tale that is told. But I've got to catch a boat. I'm doing Lear in Pittsburgh. So, what do you say? Shall we spit in our palms and shake on it? We can bring in the lawyers to mop up the blood and brains later.

SUMMERLAND
Arlitia Jones

Dramatic
Tooker, 30,

Joseph Tooker is an ambitious Chief Marshall in
1869 investigating spirit photographer William H.
Mumler's claims that he is able to photograph people
who have passed to the Other Side, or Summerland.
After visiting Mumler's studio undercover to sit for a
portrait, Tooker testifies before the judge, urging him
to go forward with a trial.

TOOKER

Yea, I have walked through the valley, Your Honor, where the
War dead covered the ground, the blue and grey of Earth's lost
armies. Death ravages without favorites. I suffered the stench
of rotting corpses, searched in vain for a place to step my foot
upon dirt not strewn with the maimed limb, crushed skull,
or shattered rib cage of my fallen brethren. Not one of them
rose up to walk beside me. Not one in a thousand. Not one in
ten thousand. The dead remain resolutely dead. Am I to believe
I saw no spirits for lack of a camera? Do not be taken in, Your
Honor. William H. Mumler is a humbug. Do not fall for his talk
of Eternal Summerland where our loved ones wait for us next
to a bubbling stream surrounded by bright flowers and birds
singing sweet melodies. Why are there birds in Eternity? Why
birds? Are there also insects? Are there Raccoons? Do not be
taken in. The sound of a gavel pounding a sound block. Your
Honor, answering the Mayor's request, I have just come from
his studio. Under false name I paid to have him make my photograph with a spirit. I made out I wished to see my dead wife.
It costs ten dollars to have your portrait made with a spirit. It
also costs ten dollars to have your portrait made without a

spirit, because sometimes the spirits miss their appointment. Mr. Mumler takes your money all the same. Or rather I should say Mrs. Mumler, takes your money. She guards the treasury and the door to the studio. Together, they are a well matched team. They pander to our wounded selves. In three days I will return to receive my printed spirit photograph and at that point I will have the evidence to submit in a formal complaint against him. I played the gullible well and I doubt he will resist the temptation to place some woebegone woman in the frame with me. You see, I have no wife dead or living. I will catch him at his game and bring clear evidence against this fabulist and there will be a trial. The dead must stay dead. The living must keep their money.

For information on this author, click on the WRITERS tab at www.smithandkraus.com

SUMMERLAND
Arlitia Jones

Dramatic
Mumler, 40

*William H. Mumler, the country's most renowned
spirit photographer in 1869, claims to be able to
photograph people in the Spirit World, or Summerland. He testifies before the judge in his well-publicized
trial, claiming his innocence and emphasizing his
calling as a Spiritualist to absolve his clients of grief.*

MUMLER

I plead innocent, Your Honor. I stand before you wrongfully
accused of fraudulent enterprise. In my own defense I claim
no occupation beyond that as an honest spirit photographer. I
alleviate grief. My process is sound and sincere. I invite you
to my studio to observe. [Beat.] Your Honor, the real argument
here is Spiritualism versus Materialism. We are debating the
nature of man's spirit. Finite? Or non-finite? Judge Dowling, if
you are a Materialist, and believe we are merely finite beings,
then we have no further discourse and you must judge me a
fraud surrounded by mere mortals who inevitably crumble
into inconsequential dust and ash. All of our loved ones have
become dust and ash. The land is covered in dust and ash. It
pains me to think of Mrs. Mumler cleaning my studio last week.
Her polishing rag brought shine to every smooth surface and
metallic fitting. If, in the end, man becomes nothing more
than finite particles of dust and ash sifting onto the furniture,
I wonder who's lost sweetheart did she set cartwheeling into
the afternoon breeze along Broadway when she leaned out the
window to shake her dust rag? *[Pause]* I am a Spiritualist, I
follow the teachings of Reverend Andrew Jackson Davis who
compels us to push back the veil between this world and the

next where our loved ones wait for us in the paradise of Summerland. Your Honor, if you are a Spiritualist like me, then it is our belief that the spirit of man, my spirit, your spirit, every spirit in this room is an infinite being that exists beyond utility of flesh and bone. It is our belief that the spirit of man is eternal, incorporate and free to communicate with the living according to the spirit's own will. It is our belief we can once more look upon the departed wife we never stopped loving, or the cherished face of the lost child we long to hold. If Summerland is where your belief leads, or at the very least your curiosity, then we have much to converse upon. The oldest and deepest mystery: What happens to us in the end? Where do we go when we die?

For information on this author, click on the WRITERS tab at www.smithandkraus.com

T

Dan Aibel

Dramatic
Jeff, late 20s

*Jeff recounts a brush with law enforcement to friend
and co-conspirator Shawn after an attack they have
commissioned sidelines the competitive rival of Jeff's
wife.*

JEFF

If I'd heard rumors. You name it. What people were saying.
"What's a salchow?" All this whack job bullshit. Does T. have
security? Gave him your card. She ever get heckled? On and on.
Next few days says should keep my ears open. And breaking off
every few minutes. To call his sergeant. Take a *whiz*. Could I sit
tight a sec he asks. *(An aside.)* Like I could say "no"? *(Resuming.)*
Guy comes back—third time—with these two FBI guys. Look
like…accountants still my heart is pounding crazy. Except they
start? Start talking? Sound like *fans*. Can't believe it. These big
goofy skating weirdos. How much she practice? Does she lift
weights? Her diet—yeah. How much *sleep* she get. Whether
she *tapes her ankles*. Finally comes out—cause I ask—they
say no good leads so far. Guy who pulled it they think did it
pretty solid. Even working up a sketch is going nowhere fast.
Descriptions full of holes and contradictions. Meanwhile
they're moaning about their boss. Telling shitty jokes. One's
got a four-year-old —asks "Too early for her to skate yet?" I'm
like "depends." *(Other side of the conversation.)* "Depends on
what?" *(Resuming.)* So I walk him through some stuff. Guy
eats it up. Three *pages* of notes he's taking. Then "Hey who's
Derrick?" Wham. Outta nowhere. Other guy. Other FBI guy.
Guy who's stood there quiet. And just says it like it's nothing.
Like it's something he's been wondering and it fits in fine with

the conversation. I said "who"? I said "Derrick?" Said "dunno." Don't know anyone off hand that I remember.

TELL HECTOR I MISS HIM
Paola Lázaro

Dramatic
Toño, 15, Puerto Rican

Toño has been kicked out of school for sexually harassing a teacher. then he has been beaten by his mother. Now, he tells Mostro, the owner of the corner store, and his wife Samira what happened.

TOÑO

Missis Vargas. English teacher. I thought she loved me Samira. I mean, El Catcher in the Rye. She showed me El Catcher in the Rye. I thought she loved me. I thought she loved me. She taught me so much. She taught me so much. Like, I think, when I think about it. I think, that nobody understood me, but her. Ella na' más. And now not even her. But, I really thought she loved me. That's why I tried what I tried. I knew she had to grade papers and she usually does it in our classroom after all the kids leave. She's not like the other teachers that go home after the day is done. She stays until she's done correcting cause I guess she doesn't want to bring the work over to home. You know? Keeping it separate? So she was gonna grade papers in our classroom after she got her café cortadito in the faculty room. I hid under her desk and then when she came back into the classroom after all the kids had left. I had a (he points to his pants) cause I usually have one all throughout her class and I sit in the front and I can smell her and this time she was even closer and I was under her so I could really smell her so I had a... And I went to touch her and I may have fallen on her- I fell on her with the... and. And she thought---- I think she thought-- I know she thought--- I was gonna you know sexually do something to her, but that's not it! That's not it! That's not what I was trying to do! I just wanted to read her a poem. She didn't wanna hear me. She didn't wanna hear it. She didn't wanna hear me. I just have a lot of energy, you know?

THREE LADIES OF ORPINGTON
Daniel Guyton

Dramatic
Marvin, 21

Marvin is a proper British gentleman in Victorian England. Here, he finally reveals the horrific truth about his life.

MARVIN

She tried to murder me, you know. On the day that I was born. She shoved a napkin inside my throat, and pinched my nose closed with her two fingers. My body turned pale, then blue. And then cold. You knew all about it. I was your child. Yours and Lord Chesterfield the Younger's. But the day that I was born... She gave me to Mr. Fennimore to... dispose of. But Mr. Fennimore didn't bury me, though, did he? Oh no, he kept me. And there I lived. And fed. And grew. The malice. And the hate. Within my heart. And even you, dear sister. Though I understand far more than most, the depravity of blaming an innocent child for the malfeasances of its mother. But there I festered. Until one day your grandpapa showed up, in dear old Mr. Fennimore's shop. Something about your grandfather's blood. Spilling out before me. Something... different... happened that day. For you see, your grandfather didn't die of old age. Or of some sad disease. Oh no, it was a letter opener, shoved deep into his abdomen. On a cold autumn day, out by the woodshed. And your grandmama paid Mr. Fennimore a visit the very same day, with 10,000 pounds for his silence. Now how do you think I could afford such beautiful clothing, mother? And Mr. Fennimore... Well, Mr. Fennimore is a rich man now. And he desires an heir. He's not a young man though. And I'm afraid he has a touch of the gout in his left leg. And a bit more than a touch in his right. So we'll have to move rather quickly on this one. So what do you say, Elenore? You can win back your entire family's estate with two words: "I do." So do you, or would you rather it all fell to ruin?

THE TROUBLE WITH CASHEWS
David MacGregor

Comic
Paul, 20s-40s

At a family gathering, Paul vents to his sister Tara as he watches their Aunt Dorothy eat from a bowl of assorted nuts and realizes that humanity is doomed.

PAUL

Just look…right over there. What do you see? Just watch her… there! She did it again! What, do you think I'm losing my mind? I know it's an old woman, sitting at a table, drinking a glass of wine, and eating some nuts from a bowl. Anyone can see that. But look more closely. Watch when she goes for a nut. And…she did it again! Seriously? You don't see it? Okay, let me ask you something. What's in that bowl? Nuts. Now, what kind of nuts? Assorted nuts. You get me? Please tell me you're beginning to understand … there! Did you see that? She's only eating the cashews! That bowl is full of assorted nuts. So, what does that typically mean? It means there's peanuts, almonds, hazelnuts, walnuts, and cashews. Does that sound about right? Now, is it just a random assortment? Equal amounts of every nut? No! It's mostly peanuts. Now, why would that be? Listen, I know you're not some kind of nut expert, but it means that peanuts must be the easiest to grow and the cheapest to harvest and people like them less than other nuts. Of all the nuts in that bowl, what kind of nut do people like the most? Cashews. Aunt Dorothy is deliberately eating only the most expensive and tastiest nuts. And the worst part? She knows what she's doing. That's why she keeps looking around to see if anyone is watching. It would be one thing if she was so out of it that she was only eating the nuts she liked best, you know, like a chimp or something. But she knows what she's doing. And it would be okay if it was just Aunt Dorothy eating all of the cashews at a family party, but there are plenty of people out there in the world just like her. People who not only want their fair share, they want everyone else's share too. In fact, do you know what we're witnessing here? The end of humanity. The total and complete destruction of human beings as a species. It may be just a bowl of nuts to you, but we are doomed. Completely and utterly doomed.

UNDERGROUND
Isla van Tricht

Seriocomic
James, early twenties

At the beginning of the play, James has just awoken and turns to the audience. What he doesn't know is that he about to have quite an adventure in the Underground.

JAMES

I have some very strong memories. You know the ones that you can smell, or taste. The ones that make you shiver. I was 11 years old, my friend's Dad put on… whichever record 'Heaven Knows I'm Miserable Now' is on…actually maybe it was the single. Anyway, I was hooked. We were sitting on a rug in his living room, and they had a cinnamon candle burning on the coffee table, I think it was almost Christmas. Whenever I hear that song now I swear I can smell cinnamon. Other Smiths songs have different smells or tastes - saliva, wine, cheesy chips, salt water, saccharine girl's perfumes blended through dull hanging cigarette smoke. I remember the first time I watched a John Hughes film, ah I fucking love John Hughes; he just gets me you know? - it was Ferris Bueller's Day Off, probably the only time I was more interested in watching a film than grabbing the tits of the girl snuggling up to me. And I've always wondered which *Breakfast Club* character I am. I always thought I wanted to be Bender, because, because he wore those leather fingerless gloves like no-one ever could. And then, don't judge me, but I kind of thought of myself as a male Allison. You know. Because of that makeover scene, I've always wanted that kind of transformation. Suddenly, like that, for people to look at me and be shocked at how much I've changed, shocked in a good way. And I don't even really mean - I mean something inside that has changed, that is so dynamic people can see it. Now, though, things are different. And somehow I think Brian has it best. He doesn't leave as part of a couple that will inevitably break it off. Let's face it, Andrew is going to drop Allison like a hot plate, and Bender will probably sell Claire's diamond earring for a pack of cigarettes. Brian, though, Brian leaves alone, but with something changed within. He's finally happy in himself, by himself. I think the most powerful thing a human being can be is to be happy by themselves, some kind of form of whole on their own. Whole and alone. That's the dream, isn't it? Besides, Brian gets the last line in the film, and we would all fucking love to have that.

VALENTINO'S MUSE
A.J. Ciccotelli

Comic
Dan, 19

*After finding a flyer for a poetry contest Dan Gardner,
a would be poet from New York City, tries to reinvent
himself as Ricardo Salome, a world class poet, and
contemplates writing a poem for the contest.*

DAN

The romantic poet waits… and waits… and waits. No happiness in his line of work. Ignorance is programmed bliss!
Eons ago, his parents said they'd castrate him if he got more
than a B in his art class, scared that he'd become a painter
and therefore a broke, homeless, drug addicted, homosexual,
alcoholic, communist atheist, who would ask them for money
perpetually, or far worse, the neighbors. Then one day his
hand picks up a pen and ka-boom! The first poem was birthed,
followed by the next and then the next. A plethora of words
all around this poet with bleeding hands like stigmata! Then
down on his knees he drops and cries to the heavens, "God,
if you have inspired me to write with no other reason but to
write, then could you give me a little talent to go along with my
drive?" God gave him far worse; he gave him writer's block.
So, this poet is named Ricardo Salome! He is me and I am he.
Perhaps some people think poets only want the approval of
others. Perhaps people are right. Fuck success! Oh, this poster
of Greece? The representation of that long faded golden age…
Where men were men and boys… frolicked naked under the
sun and wrote poems to each other. Sometimes I wonder if I'm
like those Greek boys but I snap out of it because… once there
was this boy named Farris and we used to… OH GOD SHUT
UP DAN! I mean, Ricardo! "Stuck in this man made prison of

my own device, am I! Left to the demonic forces of man-made hysteria, My mind goes asunder." Not too shabby but what does it mean? "Stuck in this..."

(Laughs at himself.)

It means I'm fucked. Perhaps life would be easier for this poet if he were born the garbage man or the paperboy. His mind would try to make stoop rhyme with... "My sadness thrown onto the stoop Isn't my life a constant droop?" No! No! No! No more. The only way I will get out of this bed is if God is willing to give his ungifted something that will rhyme with... with... That brown wooden sandal... "That brown wooden sandal Belongs to a boy named Daniel."

WASHED UP ON THE POTOMAC
Lynn Rosen

Dramatic
Mark, late twenties, a proof reader and wannabe novelist

Mark is speaking to Kate, a badass rock musician and fellow proofreader at a job where they don't matter to anyone but each other. They have a jokey, flirty work friendship, but the truth is he's secretly in love with her. On this day, a former coworker has apparently washed up dead on the Potomac. Additionally, Mark could soon be fired from his job and may never see Kate again. In this scene, Mark is in a dive bar and has just heard Kate sing for the first time. After hearing her sing, which he finds moving, and after a day where endings surround them, he's inspired to take a chance and tell Kate how he feels about her. Kate is too fearful to respond sincerely to his expression of love, so she tries to change the subject, jokingly calling him "Sugar Pops" and other silly things. He decides not to play games anymore – he gets serious – hoping she'll take a chance with him on love.

MARK

I'm not Sugar Pops! I'm Mark. Mark Aaron Colker, named for the great grandfather I never met who perished in a terrible train derailment in South America while starting a mining business. And maybe that information is not sexy or pertinent, but it's real! And I want to get real cuz I've been at this job *three years*, Kate. In three years I got all my wisdom teeth out and no one came with me and I almost got hit by a car afterward cuz of the happy gas, oh the irony, and no one knew I almost died. And my favorite teacher - the only person who believed in my writing - had a stroke and can't talk now, trapped in his body. And your father, *your father* who worked *three* jobs to get you guitar lessons died, and you're an orphan now. And my mom started looking old. And we said "Such is life" and ate pizza again. And your hair smells like the tropics. And if it weren't for you I'd go days without talking to anyone. You're my only friend, Kate. And yet, except for Pizza Palace, this is the first time in our year together that I've seen you outside the office. And my god you're even more smashing in the world. I'm tired of games. Time is finite, Kate. We are not children.

WASHED UP ON THE POTOMAC
Lynn Rosen

Dramatic
Mark, late twenties, proof reader and wannabe novelist

An intellectual with the energy of a puppy dog, Mark proofreads in a windowless office in an ad agency where no one cares about him except his fellow proofreaders, Kate, a hot musician, and Sherri, a social misfit. He attempts to write esoteric "German-like" novels but never finishes them. The day before this was disturbing: A former co-worker washed up dead on the Potomac; the proofreaders learned one of them will be fired; and Mark proclaimed his love for Kate and was rebuffed. Right before this scene, Mark realizes Sherri, 40s, has vanished mysteriously, leaving the coat and bag she always wears like armor. Sherri needed this job to get her away from her abusive mother, whereas Mark just thought of it as a job to suffer through while awaiting fame. But, if he were being honest, this job is the one place he matters. After realizing Sherri is never coming back, Mark, a good writer, is moved to write something that matters. He writes about Sherri, giving her a story of hope and promise. It's a story unlike her real life – a story he wishes for himself.

MARK
Washed Up. By Mark Aaron Colker. A true fiction. Prologue. After an act of courage and a goodbye in the only way she knew how, our potential victim- Potential *hero*, marches into the night unafraid. She goes to the Potomac. Perhaps she sits on the riverbank listening to the leaves whisper of the scope of

the world, watching the water travel where it must. She tries to capture the water in her fingers, which seem childlike in this act of folly. Perhaps she remembers her mom holding her hand when times were younger. She wants to touch everything. She wants even to be touched by the weather. She removes layers of herself - armor accumulated against a sea of intranquility - so the warm October breeze may embrace all of her - her hair, her skin, her lashes. Maybe someone will find her armor and conjure a tale about her, she thinks. Whose were these? Where is she now? In France with the birds? Our potential hero knows how she wants the story to go. She knows she has only herself. She is ready. The water roils. She genuflects before the river. She feels the brittle veins of the fallen leaves press into her knees. She doesn't mind. She sees her reflection in the water. She thinks the moonlight agrees with her. She should live in moonlight, she thinks. She wonders if anyone wonders about her. She leans in closer to her moonlit self. And what happened next? Maybe she came to a terrible conclusion that night. Or maybe, seeking a new beginning, heart pounding, heart pounding. She kept what was important -- and left the rest behind.

WELCOME TO THE WHITE ROOM
Trish Harnetiaux

Dramatic
Jennings, 40s-50s

Mr. Jennings, British, speaks to Ms. White and Mr. Paine about the dangers of a kiss.

JENNINGS

Let's think about this. Say you kiss Ms. White. Then what? Sure, momentarily you are sentinto orbit, eyes closed, lips wet, head spinning, unsure if your feet are still on the ground - thinking perhaps the two of you now occupy a different plane from the rest of reality - that you've finally found it, made it, are in a state of existence that catapults you above andbeyond the rest of normal civilization and its celestial counterparts... But wait... what then ... what's this? Once you've drawn apart and your eyes have left each other, what then I ask? I'll tell you what Paine: coldness, darkness. Ms. White will quietly turn away as she thinks fondly, only, of the first time she was kissed on the playground when she was a small child genius of six, how the boy's hand had lingered on her child waist just long enough to plant a taste of what's to come in her child brain. You'll have sudden flashes of ex-wives and satin sheets, your mind already horizontal, hovering above reason and clouded in the moment, not to clear until another front storms in and wipes away all memory of what it felt like to float for just one moment in time, to fly. And both of you, and this will only take seconds, will be deflated, dulled and de-mystified by all the power held in the suggestion of the kiss, the kinetic transcendency of what could be -- but dashed by what was.

For information on this author, click on the WRITERS tab at www.smithandkraus.com.

WHAT DIFFERENCE DOES IT MAKE?
Deb Margolin

Comic
Arnie, could be any age

Arnold Schmidt, an unemployed man, addresses the audience, as he often does throughout the play. He speaks of his wife, Myrtle, a sexy woman who is both a high-powered attorney and a cracker-jack pastry chef. The couple live in Ding A Ling A Ling Land, a made-up territory, and are both aware that they are fictional characters. Through the comic cartoon-drama, the two struggle to reconcile wildly different attitudes towards this fictional universe; Myrtle is very insulted by it, whereas Arnie's attitude is more like the eponymous title of the play: What difference does it make?

ARNIE

Myrtle and I, we're second-generation townies here; the first generation consisted of the Booble family. There was Ishkibibble Booble and his wife, Missa Booble; Ishky was a rotund man who'd lost his penis in a pickle factory, but nonetheless he and his wife had hundreds of children, many of whom came out of their mother's womb older than their mother. Ishky was one of 26 brothers, and each brother looked exactly like the others, and his job started with the same letter as his first name: Larry Booble was a Lawyer, Bob Booble was a Butcher, Dan Booble was a Doctor, and Ishky worked for IBM. Since there were hundreds of children, the Boobles had a food machine that just pushed out the food, so you could order 345 lasagnas, 19 chickens a l'orange, etc. And this sad, erudite and handsome man lived inside this machine who cooked all these menu items frantically at a small stove. One day Missa Booble let him out, and told him he had 24 hours to live his life. He exited into the dawn, and smelled flowers; it was Springtime; he walked and walked along a brook that sang to him, the sun rose over him, people smiled at him with their eyes, he ate by a river, he met a beautiful woman, jazz began to play: low, knowing jazz; he and the woman gazed at each other, told stories, laughed, fell in love, they kissed as the moon rose, they spent the night in each other's arms by the Ocean, and came the tiniest minute before dawn, the man, devastated by love and elevated by resignation, climbed back into the machine to begin his breakfast duty, never to see the sun again. This all was made up by the same weirdo who made us up!

THE WHIRLIGIG
Hamish Linklater

Comic
Derrick, early 30s

*Derrick, a fervent Red Sox fan and a baseball purist,
is watching a game on TV. He is on the phone with a
friend.*

DERRICK
No, no, NO. Ok, you wanna play that game? You wanna play
the *Blame Game*? Forget Sosa/McGwire - forget Barry Balco
Bonds - Blame the Bambino! Blame Babe-blubber butt-Ruth
for making us - for making us - will you let me finish? For
making us fall in love with the Home Run and for ruining the
integrity of a game - will you let me finish? - that was never
conceived of by Abner Doubleday to be an exhibition of *power*
- but Rather - yes I just said *rather* - an exhibition of Beauty -
yes I just said *beauty* ---- AND THIS is WHY, oh by the way,
yes, this is WHY!!! the man standing at the plate right now?
he's gonna save us, because, In Spite of *his* Power, but Because
of his Beauty - only four, this is my fifth - because he is a good,
no, a great man - while the rest of them lied, and smirked, and
had sex with Kate Hudson, and let that testosterone corrode
their souls - oh, AND ADDITIONALLY - (and this should be
incidental, but it is a perfect example so I will cite it), *because
he picked up that microphone* and walked out on the mound at
Fenway, after those marathon terrorists had tried their worst,
tried to tear us apart, and he said, and I quote, - yes my voice
is breaking a little, because I am a fucking human being, Cur-
tis, - and I quote : "This ... is our fucking city." ... I KNOW I
HAVE NEVER LEFT BERKSHIRE COUNTY - and so, *not
because* of his numbers, but BECAUSE of his spirit, his soul,
which is a beautiful one: David Ortiz, Big Papi, will be the first

player inducted into Baseball's Hall of Fame - *let me finish -* *IN SPITE* of the fact that he was a drug addict, whatever, used steroids, H.G.H. - and on cue he strikes out. No, you're right. There's no point caring any more.

For information on this author, click on the WRITERS tab at www.smithandkraus.com.

WOLF AT THE DOOR
Richard Dresser

Comic
Garth, an adult (age not important)

Garth, A Norwegian, is explaining himself to an old woman in his apartment building in New York.

GARTH

I was about to go back to Norway. But I fell in love with a Latvian. Inga. She had beautiful feet, it's what attracted me, like a rat to cheese. She was a foot model and I a cook. She moved in and we were happy. Until her brother Ivars wrote from Latvia. He needed to get out because of the Russians. She urged him to come to the USA and move in with us. He told me he couldn't work because he was missing three fingers although he always wore a mitten. I would cook fourteen hours a day at The House of Borscht and come home to cook for Inga and Ivars. One day I found them in bed together. I was puzzled but Inga explained that Ivars had been tortured by the Russians. I said, okay, good, but why the naked? She said, you have never been to Latvia. You know nothing of totalitarianism. You only know exciting recipes. One night when I brought Ivars his strudel, I told him he must at last get a job. He got angry and we ended up wrestling on the floor. I sat on him and pulled off his mitten and I saw he had all his fingers. Ah-ha! So I beat his face until he told me his dream to be a circus performer. I bought him a new suit and juggling balls and sent him off to Clown College in Florida. He graduated in the top three-quarters of his class and Inga flew down for the ceremony. But he found the circus world too political so he worked as a freelance clown, children's birthday parties, but he hated children and they hated him and it ended badly. He would lie on my sofa in my fluffy robe watching pornography and talking about how much he loved the USA and I would cook for the two of them. Inga had let her feet go so the model work dried up and I had to pay for everything: the food, the rent, Inga's vodka and Ivars' gym membership which he never once used. They went on a holiday but I couldn't go because of my work. When they arrived home they told me they had married. I said, holy cow, what kind of country is this where a sister can go to Calabasas and marry her own brother? Inga took my hand and said very gently, Garth my love, this is difficult to tell you, but Ivars is not my brother.

Rights & Permissions

AIRNESS © 2017 by Chelsea Marcantel. Reprinted by permission of Amy Mellman, ICM Partners. For performance rights, contact Di Glazer, ICM Partners, dglazer@icmpartners.com

ALL ABOUT BIFFO © 2013 by Stephen Bittrich. Reprinted by permission of Stephen Bittrich. For performance rights, contact Stephen Bittrich, sbittrich@aol.com

APROPOS OF NOTHING © 2017 by Greg Kalleres. Reprinted by permission of Greg Kalleres. For performance rights, contact Ron Gwiazda, Abrams Artists Agency, ron.gwiazda@abramsartny.com

ARCHIPELAGO © 2016 by Caridad Svich. Reprinted by permission of Caridad Svich. For performance rights, contact Caridad Svich, csvich21@caridadsvich.com

THE ARSONISTS © 2016 by Jacqueline Goldfinger. Reprinted by permission of Amy Wagner, Abrams Artists Agency. For performance rights, contact Amy Wagner, amy.wagner@abramsartny.com

THE ART OF THE FUGUE © 2017 by Don Nigro. Reprinted by permission of Don Nigro. For performance rights, contact Samuel French, Inc., 212-206-8990, www.samuelfrench.com

BLOOD AT THE ROOT © 2017 by Dominique Morisseau. Reprinted by permission of Jonathan Mills, Paradigm Agency. For performance rights, contact Samuel French, Inc., 212-206-8990, www.samuelfrench.com